P

BIBLICAL WORLDVIEW

A clear, powerful, truthful book that is critically important to internalize as you answer God's call to "bring them up in the discipline and instruction of the Lord" (Ephesians 6:4b).

David Wheaton
Author and Host, *The Christian Worldview Radio Program*

God requires all parents to instill a biblical worldview in their children's hearts and minds. Parents are in desperate need of resources to assist them in this monumental task. Dr. Josh Mulvihill provides parents, church leaders and educators with such a resource. This book will help readers understand the worldview battle that is raging for the hearts and minds of children and youth. However, it goes beyond merely identifying the problem and is an excellent primer to help those who teach children do so from a biblical worldview perspective. It is a must read for all Christians!

Dr. Glen Schultz
Author and Director, Kingdom Education Ministries

Biblical Worldview is a truth-packed, gospel-rich, easy-to-read gift to parents, grandparents, pastors and teachers. Dr. Mulvihill has created an invaluable resource we all can use to disciple our children. Josh explains the importance of shaping our children's worldview, motivated by grace, and provides the practical tools any parent or teacher can use to apply what they learn with their kids.

Marty Machowski
Pastor and Author, *Long Story Short* and *Old Story New*

Biblical
WORLDVIEW

WHAT IT IS, WHY IT MATTERS, AND HOW TO SHAPE THE **WORLDVIEW** OF **THE NEXT GENERATION**

DR. JOSH MULVIHILL

renewanation.

Produced by the Denzel Agency (www.denzel.org)

Cover and text design by Rob Williams

ISBN 978-1-951042-00-4

Printed in the United States of America

Published by

Renewanation
P.O. Box 12366
Roanoke, VA 24025
www.renewanation.org

Contact us to order:
info@renewanation.org
1-855-TO-RENEW

21 22 23 24 25 | 7 6 5 4 3 2

CONTENTS

PART 1

INTRODUCTION TO BIBLICAL WORLDVIEW

PART 2

THE BIBLICAL FOUNDATION

PART 3

THE BIBLE'S BIG STORY

FOREWORD

For more than ten years I have been on a very specific mission to see children develop a biblical worldview. It's been quite a journey as I left the pastorate and launched into this mission that God burned into my heart and mind. On this journey God has been teaching me to trust him for everything. When I first started, I had no idea how I was supposed to accomplish this work. As I have followed the leadership of the Holy Spirit, he has led me to so many key people. Dr. Josh Mulvihill is one of those people. When we first met, he was the pastor to families and children at a megachurch in Minnesota. I wondered if Josh would be someone who was chasing all the latest church fads or if he was serious about developing a biblical worldview in the children and parents in his care. I soon discovered that not only was he serious about it, he had put the programming in place to make it a reality.

Josh first joined Renewanation as a member of our Board of Directors. In the fall of 2017, he became the Executive Director of our Church and Family Ministry Division.

Together, we began to flesh out the tools we would need to effectively equip families and churches to give children a biblical worldview. We quickly agreed upon the need for a practical, introductory book on the subject.

"Biblical worldview" has been bantered around a lot over the last couple of decades, but we noticed that many Christians still don't have a grasp of its meaning. Even worse, most parents and grandparents feel ill equipped to pass on a biblical worldview in the home.

When I read the first draft of this book, I knew it was exactly what we needed. It is clear and easy to understand but not overly simple and lacking in content. It is written with the parent and grandparent in mind by a man who practices biblical worldview development in the lives of his five children every day and who implemented these teachings in a church that ministered to thousands of children and parents on a weekly basis.

This book is built around the authority and sufficiency of Scripture. At Renewanation, we unashamedly proclaim our total confidence in the Word of God. Within God's Word we discover God's good and beautiful design for the family and all areas of life. We are fully convinced that the problems the world faces today are a direct result of a failure to live according to God's good design as outlined in the Bible.

My prayer is that as you read this book you will resubmit your life and family to the authority of the Holy Scriptures. I also pray that you will engage like never before with the children God has entrusted to your care. If we are going to save this generation of children from the lies of our sin-saturated culture, we must get serious about helping our children develop a biblical worldview. Pastors, educators, parents and grandparents, will you join us in this cause? I challenge those of you who are on the front lines of the battle to do whatever it takes to raise up a new generation of young men and women who love Christ, know his ways, and are prepared to reshape our world for the glory of God.

Jeff Keaton
Founder and President of Renewanation

"I believe in Christianity as I believe that
the Sun has risen, not only because I see it,
but because by it I see everything else."

C.S. Lewis

Cornelius Van Til,
when asked why he dedicated his life to
philosophy and apologetics, once replied,
"Why, to protect Christ's little ones."

"People function on the basis of their worldview
more consistently than even they themselves realize.
The problem is not outward things.
The problem is having, and then acting upon,
the right worldview—the worldview which gives
men and women the truth of what is."

Francis Schaeffer

INTRODUCTION

Biblical worldview is vital to your work as a parent, grand-parent, pastor, or educator. It shapes your philosophy, your teaching, your counseling, your parenting, your grandparenting, and your ability to engage wisely with the world.

There is a battle being fought for the hearts and minds of children, and much is at stake. The world is working diligently to assimilate young people to its way of thinking. The beliefs our children develop inevitably shape their decisions and determine their eternal destiny. Alarmingly high numbers of Christian young people are absorbing the views of society, leaving the church, and walking away from Christ. It's time we changed that for the glory of God and for the good of our families.

Imagine the impact on homes, churches, and our nation if millions of children were given a biblical worldview. This book, *Biblical Worldview*, is an invitation to join the cause to fight the good fight of faith for the next generation. It's time for churches to elevate Bible study over the entertainment of young people, for families to prioritize discipleship over athletics or academics, and for Christian schools to prioritize maturity in Christ over college prep or academic rigor. It's time for all of us to make the Bible the foundation and focus of our ministry efforts to reach and disciple children.

What is this book about?

In a word, worldview is about beliefs. I'm passionate about shaping the beliefs of children, and you should be as well. What a child believes about Jesus will determine the child's eternal destiny. What a child believes about the Bible will impact what they believe about Jesus and will affect how the child lives. What a young person believes about gender identity, marriage and sexuality has major implications for the child and the adult they will become. What a young person believes about work, manhood, womanhood, and the social topics of our day impacts the decisions and direction of a child's life. This book will equip you to help young people develop a strong biblical foundation and doctrinal framework for a biblical worldview.

Biblical worldview is a set of beliefs about life that determines how we live. A biblical worldview will help children develop a deep, lasting, and culture-transforming faith in Christ. It should be no surprise that many young people call themselves Christians, but think and live in a non-Christian way. Young people will resemble a godless society if they do not have a biblically-based, Jesus-centered, and God-driven worldview.

Biblical worldview is built on the foundation of the authority, inerrancy, and sufficiency of the Bible. This book will help you establish this foundation in the hearts and minds of young people so that they trust the Bible, think about life from a Christian perspective, and live according to biblical principles. Scripture is *the* source that shapes our views about God and his world and must be the focus for worldview development. We take our principles and practices from God's Word, not the world. When the world's meaning, messages, and methods become assimilated into raising the next generation, we shouldn't be surprised when children look more like the world than like Christ.

Our worldview is developed as we establish beliefs about four critical topics:

- **Creation**: How did I get here? What is my purpose?
- **Rebellion**: What went wrong? Why is there evil and suffering?
- **Salvation**: What is the solution? Where do I find hope?
- **Restoration**: What happens in the future? How do we transform lives and change the world?

These four pillars create the framework for a person's worldview. It is critical that all four pillars of faith are firmly established and that deep-down convictions are developed around these biblical truths.

Biblical Worldview is a serious call to shape the next generation's beliefs with the Bible. The aim of biblical worldview is embracing gospel truth for godly living. This book is a short introduction to biblical worldview and will equip you to help children develop a biblically-based view of life that will transform their homes, communities, and nations.

Who is this book for?

I wrote this book for parents, grandparents, pastors, and educators. When biblical worldview is talked about, many individuals have a vague idea of the concept, but do not have a concrete understanding of what biblical worldview is or why it matters. Many pastors have heard of biblical worldview, but believe it is an academic activity with little applicability to the church. Nothing could be further from the truth. The vast majority of Christian parents and grandparents desire to raise children with a firm biblical foundation that will lead to lifelong faith in Jesus and a fruitful ministry serving him in the world. Despite the desire, low numbers of parents and grandparents nurture their child's faith, and few have any intentional plan. Many Christian schools have not integrated the Bible into classrooms or curriculum and are not training children to think biblically. This book reveals how vitally important biblical worldview is for the church, home, and school, and shows how to help a young person develop a biblical worldview.

Every Christian parent and grandparent must help children develop a biblical worldview. Every pastor and Christian educator should equip the family to disciple the next generation with a biblical worldview. This book will help you do that.

Overview of the book

Biblical Worldview contains three sections: (1) an introduction to biblical worldview; (2) a biblical foundation to develop strong doctrinal beliefs about the Bible; and (3) a framework for biblical worldview based on the big story of the Bible. In part 1, we'll explore why worldview matters, what it is, and the five influences that shape the beliefs of young people. In part 2, we will study key truths about the Bible that should be taught to every young person to establish its authority, prove its reliability, show its trustworthiness, and apply its usefulness to all of life. A child's views about the Bible will shape the child's views about life. We will end the second part by exploring six ways to help children live the Word of God. The final section of the book provides a framework for biblical worldview by teaching the big story of the Bible in four words and corresponding outlines so that the information can be taught to children. The book concludes with resources to help a young person develop a biblical worldview

One of the greatest challenges with the worldview discussion is the academic way the subject is approached. The most common approach is to address the subject from a philosophical starting point with terminology that makes a person's head spin and causes people to question the applicability of the subject to everyday life. Let me assure you, this is not an invalid approach. It just doesn't resonate with the average Christian, who reads academic-sounding words and a litany of terms that end with "ism" and automatically thinks, "Not interested." I believe biblical worldview needs to begin with the Bible, focus on the Bible, and apply the Bible to life.

Consider this book the CliffsNotes on the subject, an easy-to-read, packs-a-gospel-punch, high-view-of-Scripture kind of book. It's not meant to be exhaustive, but introductory. It will introduce you to biblical worldview and do so in a way that will encourage you to think deeply about its priority in life and ministry and will equip you to make a real and lasting difference as you reach and disciple young people today. This book will help you understand what biblical worldview is, why it's important, and how to help a young person develop a biblical worldview.

Dr. Josh Mulvihill

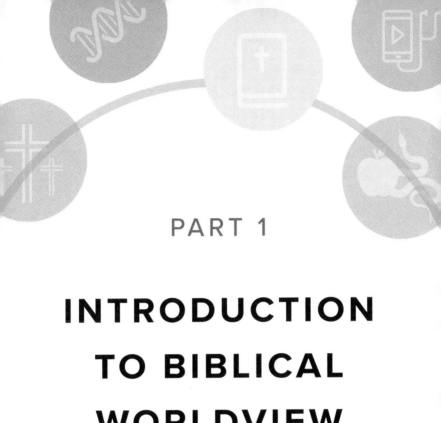

PART 1

INTRODUCTION TO BIBLICAL WORLDVIEW

I

WHY WORLDVIEW MATTERS

SIX REASONS EVERY CHILD NEEDS A BIBLICAL WORLDVIEW

Every Christian parent, grandparent, and pastor I know wants to see the children they love grow up to know, love, and follow Jesus for a lifetime. We want our children to smell like the scent of heaven and to spend eternity there.

Unfortunately, many Christian young people are unprepared to navigate the tidal wave of unbiblical ideas that confront them. We all know teenagers who have drifted and walked away from Christ. We never like to think our own child could one day be that person. When the pressure is turned up, our children will struggle if they do not have the confidence that comes from knowing what they believe and why they believe it.

We are losing our children to the world at an alarming rate. Evangelical churches pride themselves on an attractional model that attempts to reach seekers with the gospel while our children are evangelized into secular humanistic thought by the very people we are trying to reach. Who is doing a better job evangelizing children, the world or the church? If we are honest, many churches are struggling to pass on a deep, lasting, Bible-shaped faith to future generations.

Parents and grandparents want the best for children, yet passions and priorities are often out of order. Athletics and academics are often prioritized over the nurture of a child's faith. Children may end up at a prestigious university or receive an athletic scholarship, but their faith lags far behind and leaves them vulnerable to the deception of the world. Barna research has found that "a person's worldview is primarily shaped and is firmly in place by the time someone reaches the age of thirteen; it is refined through experience during the teen and early adult years; and then it is passed on to others during their adult life. Such studies underscore the necessity of parents and other influencers being intentional in how they help develop the worldview of children."[1] High numbers of parents and grandparents are not developing their child's worldview, and the spiritual vacuum is being filled by cultural ideas and secular thought.

That's why *worldview matters*. That phrase describes my message to parents, grandparents, pastors, and educators. Biblical worldview is worthy of our attention and resources.

Here are six reasons why every family, church, and school needs to help children develop a biblical worldview.

1. To provide wisdom for life

When you have a parenting problem, where do you look for answers? When you want to learn how to grandparent, where do you turn for guidance? When you want teaching methods, where do you look for ideas? When you have a decision to make, where do you turn for wisdom?

The Bible claims to provide everything needed for salvation in Jesus, growth into Christlikeness, obedience to God's commands, and godly living. The reformers called this *sola Scriptora,* which translates to "Scripture alone" and is the foundation for the doctrine of sufficiency. The doctrine of sufficiency is found in 2 Timothy 3:15–17 (emphasis added), "the sacred writings, which are able to make you wise for salvation through faith in Christ Jesus … and *equipped for every good work.*" Peter makes the same claim when he says that God, "has given us *everything* we need for life and godliness" (2 Peter 1:3 GW, emphasis added). The key word in these verses is *everything.* God has given us everything we need in Scripture to do what he has commanded us in the Bible.

One of the most urgent needs for Christians today is to reclaim the sufficiency of Scripture for all of life. James Montgomery Boyce makes a similar observation:

> In Martin Luther's day, *sola Scriptura* had to do with the Bible being the sole ultimate authority for

Christians over against challenges to it from the traditions of the medieval church, church councils, and the Pope. The Reformers wanted Scripture to stand alone as the church's true authority. Today, at least in the evangelical church, that is not our chief problem; we assert biblical authority. Rather, our problem is in deciding whether the Bible is sufficient for the church's life and work. We confess its authority, but we discount its ability to do what is necessary to draw unbelievers to Christ, enable us to grow in godliness, provide direction for our lives, and transform and revitalize society. … In other words, in the sixteenth century the battle was against those who wanted to add church traditions to Scripture, but in our day the battle is against those who would have us use worldly means to do God's work.[2]

Using worldly means to do God's work. That is an unfortunate statement, but a common reality. Families look to psychology to help them raise children instead of the Bible. Pastors import business practices while pragmatism drives decisions rather than the methodology of Scripture. Christian schools utilize secular textbooks instead of Bible-based curriculum. Psychology, pragmatism, and secular textbooks are symptoms of a deeper theological problem that results from an underdeveloped grasp of the sufficiency of Scripture and leads to replacing the authority of the Bible with another source. When it comes to parenting, grandparenting, education, and the church, will we look to the Bible for our instruction or to another source?

The Bible contains all that we need to know God, grow into Christlike maturity, and obey his commands. The Bible does not exclusively address every field or topic, but when the Bible speaks on a subject it is authoritative.

2. To develop the foundation for lifelong faith in Jesus

Perhaps you've heard about the high number of young people who are dropping out of the church, walking away from their faith in Christ, and the low numbers of young believers who have a biblical view of life. I've been a pastor to families for nearly twenty years and have seen the following patterns develop:

- *Biblical illiteracy*: Alarmingly high numbers of children raised in Christian homes do not know *what* the Bible teaches.
- *Biblical confusion*: High numbers of young Christians do not know *why* they should believe the teachings of the Bible instead of other views.
- *Biblical immaturity*: When young people encounter a different belief system, many do not know *how* to defend their faith or explain the basic truths of the Bible.

What leads to lifelong faith for children? According to the apostle Paul, a Scripture-saturated, Bible-based upbringing shapes the beliefs of children. Paul instructs Timothy to "continue in what you have learned and have firmly believed, knowing from whom you learned it, and how from childhood you have been acquainted with the sacred writings" (2 Tim. 3:14–15).

One of Paul's goals for Timothy is firm belief, which is the result of three things: *what* Timothy learned (biblical truth), *who* he learned from (parent, grandparent, and spiritual mentor), and *how* he learned (being taught the Bible from childhood). Notice, the Bible is concerned with *what* children learn, *who* teaches children, and *how* children are to learn. If we want children to live a godly life, for their entire life, then these are God's methods toward that end. Scores of Christian children have not been taught the Scriptures, leaving them susceptible to false teaching, immaturity, and unbelief.

3. To shape character and conduct by truth

A common phrase used to communicate how to pass on faith to future generations is, "Faith is caught not taught." It sounds spiritual. Unfortunately, it's unbiblical. The Bible elevates both as important. Faith is caught, which is why we must be able to say to young people, "Imitate me as I imitate Christ" (1 Cor. 11:1 GW). Faith is also taught. The Bible prioritizes teaching as the primary method of helping future generations know Christ and grow in maturity. Let's explore a few passages (emphases added) that command parents and grandparents to teach the truth of God's Word to young people.

- *"Teach* these things to your children and your children's children" (Deut. 4:9).
- "You shall *teach* them diligently to your children, and shall *talk* of them when you sit ... walk ... lie down ... when you rise" (Deut. 6:7).
- "He commanded our [grand]fathers to *teach* their children, that the next generation might know them, the children yet unborn, and arise and tell them to their children" (Ps. 78:5–6).
- "Hear, my son, your father's *instruction* and forsake not your mother's *teaching*" (Prov. 1:8).
- "Fathers, do not provoke your children to anger, but bring them up in the discipline and *instruction* of the Lord" (Eph. 6:4).
- "Older women ... are to *teach* what is good, and so train the young women to love their husbands and children, to be self-controlled, pure, working at home, kind and submissive to their own husbands. ...[Older men] *urge* the younger men to be self-controlled" (Titus 2:3–6).

Parents and grandparents are to use the Bible to shape who a child becomes and how the child lives. This is the pattern and command of Scripture. Parents and grandparents in Deuteronomy were commanded to teach the law of God (Ten Commandments) to children so that future generations would develop an understanding of right and wrong. The father and mother in Proverbs provide an example of how to train children to develop a biblical view of life as they instruct their son to make wise choices about friendship (1:10), money (3:9), marriage (5:18), work (6:6), and more. The grandparents of Titus 2 shape future generations by providing character training and guidance on how to be a godly mother and wife.

4. To defend against counterfeit ideas

A biblical worldview helps children defend their faith. Raising children today requires a Colossians 2:6–8 mindset, "As you received Christ Jesus the Lord, so walk in him, rooted and built up in him and established in the faith, just as you were taught, abounding in thanksgiving. See to it that no one takes you captive by philosophy and empty deceit, according to human tradition, according to the elemental spirits of the world, and not according to Christ."

Our strategy is simple and contains two steps. We are to teach the core truth of Scripture so that a Christian is established in faith, then introduce a competing belief system and dismantle it by exposing why it is false. When I teach kids, I refer to this as the Bible's big truth and the world's big lie.

What are the most prominent philosophies that children are exposed to today? Listen for buzzwords, repetitive phrases, and popular ideas of the day. Familiarize yourself with them, learn what they teach and why they are deficient, and be able to point out these arguments when you see them in education, media, or culture. In a post-Christian society children are going to face strong opposition and competing belief systems, and unless they are rooted in the Bible they will absorb the ideas of our day and assimilate to the beliefs of our culture. Our aim is to shape the beliefs of young people, and to do that we must train children to defend their faith against deceptive and competing belief systems. Biblical worldview is an effective evangelism tool to answer questions and proclaim the gospel.

5. To answer the big questions of life

A biblical worldview answers the big questions that children ask, such as, *Where did I come from? Why am I here? Who am I? What went wrong with the world? What is the solution? What is the purpose of life? What happens in the future?*

Young people are hungry for truth and are searching for answers. They desire open and honest face-to-face conversations. Young people want real answers and are attracted to authenticity. Due to an overabundance of information, young people do not know what information is trustworthy, so they have a prove-it-to-me mindset. One of the most compelling proofs for young people is an authentic life that is faithful to Scripture. The individual that speaks truth in love and practices what he or she preaches is incredibly influential in a young person's life. Here are three suggestions to answer the spiritual questions children will have:

- *Ask questions before children ask them.* Don't be afraid to talk about difficult topics. Encourage children to think deeply about the truths of the Bible.
- *Answer with Scripture.* Encourage children to become students of God's Word, so that they either know the answer or know where to get the answer.
- *Aim to be an askable parent, grandparent, pastor, or teacher.* Invite questions, take them seriously, and answer them diligently so that the child who is weighing the claims of the Bible will be persuaded to believe in Christ.

6. To equip individuals for service to Christ

The world does not need Christians who are culturally saturated. It needs agents of the gospel filled with the aroma of Christ. A biblical worldview not only shapes what a child believes, but also equips the child to live in a manner worthy of the gospel, for the good of others and for the glory of God through their future vocation. A biblical view of topics such as science, law, medicine, and education will provide the framework for children to positively impact the world for Christ.

A biblical worldview equips children to serve God using the gifts he has given them. God didn't just save us from something, he saved us for something—to resume the task for which we were originally created. We bring him glory when we reflect his character to others. Running a business, teaching students, or managing a home are not secondary activities, but doing God's work in the world. A child's future vocation is not something he or she does for God; it is a way to participate in God's work.

The importance of the early years

Paul addresses the importance of the early years in salvation and spiritual growth when he writes to Timothy, "and how from *childhood* you have been acquainted with the sacred writings, which are able to make you wise for salvation through faith in Christ Jesus" (2 Tim. 3:15, emphasis added). The psalmist states, "O God, from my *youth* you have taught me" (Ps. 71:17, emphasis added). The early years are critically important, and we must not buy into the lie that children are too young to handle the deep truths of Scripture and wait to teach children the whole counsel of God's Word.

James Montgomery Boice recognized that the habits of youth often become the habits of adulthood. He states, "The decisions of youth form habits that guide us from that point on and are hard to break. If we form good habits when we are young—reading the Bible, spending time in prayer, enjoying the company of God's people, going to church, rejecting sin, and practicing to be honest and do good— these habits will go with us through life and make good choices later in life easier. If on the contrary we make bad choices, later we will find good choices harder to make and the bad habits nearly impossible to break."[3]

J.C. Ryle, an English pastor who lived from 1816 to 1900, has a strong warning for all parents and grandparents to heed. "What young men will be, in all probability depends on what they are now, and they seem to forget this. Youth is the planting time of full age, the molding season in the little space of human life, the turning point in the history of man's mind. By the shoot that springs up we can judge the type of tree that is growing, by the blossoms we judge the kind of fruit, by the spring we judge the type of harvest coming, by the morning we judge the coming day, and by the character of the young man, we may generally judge what he will be when he grows up."[4]

Ryle continues,

"I say it because experience tells me that people's hearts are seldom changed if they are not changed when young. Seldom indeed are men converted when they are old. Habits have deep roots. Once sin is allowed to settle in your heart, it will not be turned out at your bidding. Custom becomes second nature, and its chains are not easily broken. The prophet has well said, 'Can the Ethiopian change his skin, or the leopard its spots? Neither can you do good who are accustomed to doing evil' (Jeremiah 13:23). Habits are like stones rolling down hill—the further they roll, the faster and more ungovernable is their course. Habits, like trees, are strengthened by age. A boy may bend an oak when it is a sapling—a hundred men cannot root it up when it is a full grown tree. A child can wade over the Thames River at its fountainhead— the largest ship in the world can float in it when it gets near the sea. So it is with habits: the older the stronger—the longer they have held possession, the harder they will be to cast out. They grow with our growth, and strengthen with our strength. Custom is the nurse of sin. Every fresh act of sin lessens fear and remorse, hardens our hearts, blunts the edge of our conscience, and increases our evil inclination.[5]

If you are discouraged by these comments due to an adult child or older family member who has not embraced Christ, then I want to remind you that there is always hope for transformation in Christ. The Scriptures are full of individuals who trusted Christ later in life—such as the prodigal son who returned home, Nicodemus, who sought Christ to be born again when he was old, and the thief who trusted Christ at the end of life—so no man need despair. If you are prone to worry, the Bible reminds you that the remedy is to trust God and bring your burden to the Lord in prayer (Phil. 4:6–7).

Research creates additional urgency as to the importance of the early years in the discipleship of young people. A survey of the members of the National Association of Evangelicals (NAE) found that 63 percent became a Christian between the ages of four and fourteen, with the median age being eleven.[6] The same survey also found that 34 percent became a Christian between the age of fifteen and twenty-nine. According to this study, 97 percent of NAE members became a Christian *before* the age of 30.

A child's belief system, his or her worldview, is almost fully formed by the age of twelve. Before a child becomes a teenager, his or her understanding of the world, views of God, perspectives about morality, convictions about Jesus, and a long list of other topics is nearly complete.

Delaying doctrinal training, abdicating discipleship to pastors or schools, or avoiding difficult topics is a recipe for spiritual disaster. It is important to note that beginning early is not a guarantee that a child will embrace Christ or live biblically, as it is the power of the gospel, not the correct methods, that changes hearts. However, we are wise to recognize and utilize the patterns and principles of Scripture and resources that help us shape the beliefs of the next generation.

Biblical worldview matters. It is worthy of your time and attention. Worldview matters because every child is in the process of developing their beliefs about God, creation, sin, hell, salvation, marriage, sex and a long list of other topics. Their beliefs on these topics determine their life decisions and eternal destination. Let us commit to train children to think and live biblically. My goal in this book is to equip you to do that.

2

WHAT IS BIBLICAL WORLDVIEW?

Creation. Marriage. Divorce. Jesus. Gender. Education. Abortion. Parenting. Islam. Immigration. Vaccines. The Bible. Climate change. Did any of these words generate a response in your mind? Did you silently state agreement or disagreement as you read some of the words? Did any personal convictions well up inside you? How about when I turn some of these words into questions?

- Does the Bible contain errors?
- What is marriage?
- Is divorce ever permissible?
- What is the role of government?
- Is gender determined by biology or by choice?
- What is the purpose of education?
- Do vaccines cause autism?

Your answer to each of these questions represents a portion of your worldview. Every person has a worldview. Worldview is a way of summarizing what we believe to be true, which determines how we live. If we believe vaccines cause autism, we don't vaccinate our children. If we believe a person's gender is discovered rather than predetermined, then we encourage children to explore their gender identity to learn who they are. If we believe divorce is not an option, we work through conflict and commit to lifelong faithfulness in marriage.

What you believe about vaccines, gender, and divorce leads to very real consequences for children. The same could be said about a long list of topics. The point is this: *Our beliefs matter and that's why worldview matters.*

Worldview has been defined in many different ways. The most common is to refer to worldview as a lens through which we view the world. While this view is helpful conceptually, it is not descriptive enough to help us fully understand the topic. It gives the false impression that changing worldviews is as easy as putting on a new pair of glasses, which, of course, it is not.

Worldview has also been defined as an explanation and interpretation of the world and an application of this view to life. This is an intellectual way of saying worldview is what you believe and how you live.

Biblical worldview is a set of beliefs, assumptions, or values based on the Bible that determines how a person lives. The goal of worldview training is to shape beliefs with the Bible to equip a young person to apply God's truth to life for the good of others and the glory of God. A complete biblical worldview is the gospel. A Christian worldview is based on the Bible's big story. A biblical worldview is developed by teaching young people the whole counsel of the Word of God and living as a Christlike example worthy of imitation. It is not an abstract, academic discipline that is concerned with winning arguments or proving intellect. Biblical worldview is a way to summarize the life-changing truths of Scripture, with a laser focus on the gospel.

I summarize biblical worldview in four words: *creation, rebellion, salvation, and restoration.* These four biblical truths create the framework that enables a young person's faith to be "rooted and built up in Christ" rather than destroyed by human ideas (Col. 2:7-8). They also answer the big questions of life.

- *Creation: **God made the world good*** (Gen. 1:1). God is the sole source of all things (Col. 1:16). God created everything for his glory and our enjoyment. Where did the world come from? What is my purpose in life? What does it mean to be human? What is God's design for manhood and womanhood? What is marriage?
- *Rebellion: **Sin made the world groan*** (Rom. 3:23). There was a great rebellion against the Creator resulting in sin, which distorts our ability to understand the world apart from God's restoring grace (Gen. 3; Rom. 3:23). Sin makes

us blind and deaf. Sin brought the entire world under a curse, separates us from God, and results in eternal punishment for those who reject Christ. What is true? What is sin? What is wrong with the world? Why do I suffer?

- **_Salvation: Jesus paid the penalty for sin_** (John 3:16). Jesus died on the cross to pay the penalty for sin. Jesus is the way, the truth, and the life. He reversed the effects of the fall. We are called to walk in obedience and not to be conformed to the world, but be transformed by the renewing of the mind (Rom. 12:1–2). Our goal is Christlike maturity (Col. 1:28–29) and training for godliness (1 Tim. 4:7). What is the solution to the world's problems? What is the gospel? Who is Jesus? What must a person do to be saved? What is discipleship? How do I make wise choices? How should I live?

- **_Restoration: God will make the world new_** (2 Cor. 5:17). Jesus conquered sin and death. We have hope in the living God who will restore all things and create a new heaven and earth where he reigns forever with no more pain or sadness (Rev. 21:5). God didn't just save us _from_ something, he also saved us _for_ something—to resume the task for which we were originally created. We serve God by using the gifts he gave us. We bring him glory when we reflect his character to others. Living in light of eternity reminds us that life has a greater purpose than our own happiness. Joy is found when we love and obey Jesus. How can I be happy? Where do I find hope and joy? What happens after death? Is there anything worth living for? How should I use my time, talents, and treasures?

The secularized world aggressively opposes these foundational truths and is actively trying to convince young people to embrace a different belief system—one that will ultimately destroy their faith in Christ. Children are confronted with a secular worldview on a daily basis through media, from peers, and in education, which can be summarized as secular humanism (man is god) with a growing appreciation for socialism (government is god). Humanism replaces God's big story with these four words: *naturalism, relativism, atheism, and materialism.* If the world's big lies are internalized they become faith-busting beliefs, and young people walk away from Jesus.

Biblical worldview is concerned with knowing the truth and living in accordance with it. Pilate asked Jesus a question, perhaps the most important question of all time: "What is truth?" Truth is the correct account of reality, which comes from God. By contrast, Satan is known as the father of lies who seeks to deceive and destroy. The Christian believes six things about truth:

1. *Truth exists.* It is real. It is not determined by an individual or majority consensus. Truth

exists whether a person believes it or not. The psalmist states, "The sum of your word is truth, and every one of your righteous rules endures forever" (Ps. 119:160).

2. *Truth is knowable.* John 8:32 states, "You will know the truth, and the truth will set you free."

3. *All truth comes from God and bears witness to him.* When a person discovers truth, they are on a path to discover the Creator of truth.

4. *Truth is eternal.* It does not change and is not created. Jesus states, "Heaven and earth will pass away, but my words will never pass away" (Matt. 24:35 NIV).

5. *Truth is a person.* Jesus said of himself, "I am the way, and the truth, and the life. No one comes to the Father except through me" (John 14:6).

6. *The Bible is the final authority on truth.* The Bible functions as a measuring stick, the standard of truth, and the norm against which human thoughts and ideas are to be tested (1 Thess. 5:21). All knowledge claims and beliefs must be shaped by the Bible and come under its scrutiny. The Bible is our plumb line.

If we want children to know the Truth, live according to the Way, and have eternal life, then worldview should matter to us. Worldview is discipleship that shapes what a young person believes, how he or she lives, and where each child will spend eternity. Worldview's main focus is the evangelism and discipleship of young people. The question is who is evangelizing and discipling your child and what beliefs are shaping them?

What is your worldview?
Many Christian adults don't have a distinctly Christian worldview. An important question to ask yourself is, *Does my way of looking at the world correspond to the world as it is according to God in the Bible?* We cannot provide a biblical worldview to a child if we do not have one ourselves. While this book is intended to train you to help a child develop a biblical worldview, the starting point for you may be the development of your own biblical worldview.

To understand the worldview of your child, consider three questions:

- *What does your child believe to be true?* Do you know what your child believes about the Bible, Jesus, marriage, gender, hell, and salvation? It should be the goal of every parent, grandparent, pastor, and teacher to shape the beliefs of children from the Bible.
- *What authority shapes those beliefs?* Every child will look to an authority to determine truth. The authority the child chooses will determine

what the child believes and how the child lives.
While there are many sources of authority that
individuals look to, some of the most common
include science, psychology, government, cultural norms, or the Bible.

- *How does your child live?* Just because a child
  knows the right answer doesn't mean the
  child has embraced Christ or believes the Bible.
  A child's behavior reveals his or her true beliefs.
  Pay careful attention to a child's passions
  and priorities as well as the fruit of the
  child's actions.

One of the central aims of biblical worldview training
is to shape the beliefs of young people using the Bible
(2 Tim. 3:16). The Bible talks about the importance of
helping young people learn biblical truth to establish firm
beliefs (2 Tim. 3:14–15), and to avoid deceptive philosophy
which leads to wrong living (Col. 2:8, 20–23). The Bible
also says a child should receive a parent's instruction
so he or she is not enslaved by sin (Prov. 1:8–10; 3:5–7),
and listen to a grandparent's teaching, which leads to hope
in Christ and lifelong obedience to God (Psalm 78:4–8).

We must train young people to love God's Word, trust
God's Word, and live by God's Word. A child may not
know the answer, but if we teach a child to study the Bible,
he will know where to look to find the answer. A biblical
worldview is developed as we train young people to ask the
question, "What does the Bible say about ____?"

Many young Christians are not adequately prepared to handle the tidal wave of secular views presented to them and they are often left to discern for themselves if what they hear is true. The combination can be lethal for children who are naturally trusting, unsure of the Bible's teachings, and lack strong voices that speak God's truth. As a result, many children absorb an unbiblical worldview even while they seek to follow Christ.

Much is at stake. Every child's eternal destiny depends on what he or she believes about Jesus. The major life decisions every child makes are determined by their beliefs, such as the ones at the beginning of this chapter. The missionary zeal of our culture is operating at full force. We have the critical job of discipling children with a biblical worldview, which happens as we integrate the Bible into everything we do in our home, church, and school. Unless children are well grounded in Scripture, they will look more like the culture than like Christ. Children need the soul-gripping, life-shaping words of Scripture to develop a deep, lasting, and culture-transforming faith.

3

WHO SHAPES
A CHILD'S WORLDVIEW?

EXPLORING THE FIVE GREATEST
INFLUENCERS IN THE LIFE OF A CHILD

Who are the most influential people in a young person's life? A Barna study wanted to know the answer to a similar question and asked 602 teenagers, "Who, besides your parents, do you admire most as a role model?"[1] According to Barna, the top five influences in the life of young people are (1) parents, (2) other family members, typically grandparents, (3) teachers and coaches, (4) friends, and (5) pastors or religious leaders.

After parents, the next greatest potential influence in the life of a child is a grandparent, not a teacher, not a peer, not a pastor. The top two influences in the life of a child are both found in the home, which reminds us that God designed family discipleship as the primary means to help a young person know, love, and serve Jesus. The third most impactful influence on young people are educators. After the family, education has become the greatest spiritual influence on young people. Peers hold the fourth place on the list, suggesting that their influence is perceived to be greater than it actually is. The church holds the fifth place of influence in the life of a young person. This finding does not minimize the God-ordained role of the church, but it does remind us that we must expand our vision of discipleship beyond the walls of the church.

When teenagers were asked why they named a particular person as influential, they provided the following reasons: The person was worthy of imitation; they wanted to follow in the footsteps of the chosen person; they were there for the teenager; and they were interested in the teenager's future. For better or worse, young people are imitating the people they know best and who care for them.

It may sound simplistic, but the greatest influencers of young people are typically those who invest the greatest amount of time into their life. When I look at Barna's five influences it follows that logic. The five greatest influencers are the people who spend the most time with young people over the course of their life.

Children absorb beliefs from those around them beginning in the earliest days of life. A person's beliefs are generally unconscious and inherited. Children become who they spend time with. Thus, we would be wise to be selective about whom our children spend time with and to pay careful attention to our own lives so that we can say to a young person, "Imitate me as I imitate Christ" (1 Cor. 11:1). Let's explore the five greatest influences in the life of a child.

Home + Church

God created two great commission institutions for the evangelism and discipleship of children: the church and the home. Biblically, education is a parent's responsibility and does not exist as its own institution. The church is given a supporting role. It is to equip the home to educate a child.

- *The family:* God gave parents and grandparents the primary and secondary role of disciple-making. The psalmist provides a multigenerational vision for our family: "so that they should set their *hope in God* [evangelism] and not forget the works of God, but *keep his commandments* [discipleship]; and that they should not be like their fathers, a stubborn and rebellious generation" (Ps. 78:7–8). The goal of parenting and grandparenting is salvation and sanctification of children as well as maturity into the likeness of Christ (Col. 1:28–29).
- *The church:* God gave churches the role of equipping families to disciple children. "Go therefore and make disciples of all nations, baptizing them in the name of the Father and of the Son and of

the Holy Spirit, teaching them to observe all
that I have commanded you" (Matt. 28:19–20).
Making disciples begins at home, then moves
across the street, and around the world.

- *The school:* God has given parents the responsibility to teach children, and that happens for
many families today in partnership with educational organizations. "A student [disciple] is not
above his teacher, but everyone when he is fully
trained will be like his teacher" (Luke 6:40).
- *Media:* Media is a strong influence on the beliefs
of children, but because media is not an
ordained institution by God or a person, it is
beyond the scope of this chapter. *The Tech-Wise
Family* by Andy Crouch offers excellent guidance on this topic.

One of the most famous disciples in the Bible is Timothy and it is helpful to note the influences that shaped
him into a man of God. In 2 Timothy 3:14–15, Paul states
that Timothy's firm belief was the result of *what* he
learned, *how* he learned, and *who* he learned from. Who
did Timothy learn from? Timothy provides an example of
discipleship in Scripture combining the influences of
parent (Eunice), grandparent (Lois), and spiritual mentor
(Paul) (2 Tim. 1:5). When a child has all three spiritual
influences there is a greater chance for lifelong faith. We
know the powerful influence of a father and grandfather,
but this passage also shows that when God's ideal does not

occur a child can still grow up to know, love, and serve Christ.

Many well-intentioned families and church leaders have a theology of discipleship that does not reflect the pattern or practice of Scripture. For the past fifty years, many pastors have operated as if the church were the number one influence in the life of children, and have done little to equip parents while ignoring grandparents and education. Let us align our discipleship practices with Scripture and implement a strategy to reach and disciple young people that is built around parents, grandparents, teachers, and the church.

INFLUENCES THAT SHAPE THE BIBLICAL WORLDVIEW OF CHILDREN

1. Parents

It takes a family to develop a biblical worldview. Perspectives about life and views of the world are primarily formed at home during childhood and adolescence. It is a parent and grandparent, not a pastor or educator, who God has designed to primarily disciple a child. The church and school are important partners toward this end, but their role is supportive and not to be substituted for the home.

According to the Bible, parents have been given the primary role of discipling children to maturity in Christ. Consider the following passages that speak about the God-designed role parents have in passing on a heritage of faith to future generations:

- "You shall teach them diligently to your children, and shall talk of them when you sit in your house, and when you walk by the way, and when you lie down, and when you rise (Deut. 6:7).
- "We will tell the next generation the praise-worthy deeds of the LORD, his power, and the wonders he has done" (Ps. 78:1–8 NIV).
- "Hear, my son, your father's instruction, and forsake not your mother's teaching" (Prov. 1:8).
- "Fathers ... bring [your children] up in the discipline and instruction of the Lord" (Eph. 6:4).

Research reveals that parents know it's their job to disciple a child, yet this understanding has not translated to sustained activity at home. A Barna study states: "A majority of parents do not spend any time during a typical week discussing religious matters or studying religious materials with their children. ... Parents typically have no plan for the spiritual development of their children; do not consider it a priority, have little or no training in how to nurture a child's faith."[2] Most parents lack a biblical, God-honoring plan and have a home that is light on discipling.

Parents, if this is you, I don't write this to make you feel guilty. Sometimes we need a gracious reminder to motivate us to action. Our children are going to be discipled by someone. If we are not doing the discipling, others will disciple them, and there is a good likelihood they will develop unbiblical beliefs and lifestyles. If you are not regularly reading the Bible at home, discussing issues based on the Bible, and nurturing a child's faith, then this needs to be your primary area of growth.

As a parent, what you do is important, but even more important is who you are. Deuteronomy 4:9 tells parents to "watch yourself closely" and then "teach children." The combination of an imitatable faith plus the habit of teaching and training our children is powerful. Hypocrites rarely produce the results they desire. Studies have found that the more a parent's walk matches their talk, the greater the likelihood of a child following Christ. A large study of more than 5,000 atheists found this to be the greatest predictor that determines why children in Christian homes walk away from Christ: "The less parents 'walk the walk' about religious beliefs, the more likely their children are to walk away."[3] The influence of a parent is powerful.

Family discipleship

Alarmingly high numbers of young people have never been discipled. Young people have bits and pieces of the truth, but have never been taught the Bible comprehensively. As a result, they lack a biblical worldview. For example, almost every young person raised in a Christian home knows that Christ died for them, but many are unable to articulate the doctrines of Christ's death such as justification, redemption, propitiation, and reconciliation. Children need to know the key people, themes, and stories of the Bible as well as the core doctrines of

Christianity. Children also need to be trained to think biblically about economics, justice, friendship, gender, and matters of life.

It is important to help young people see that Christianity is a comprehensive way of living. Young people are taught that spiritual things help on Sunday morning and apply to salvation, but not how they translate into their everyday lives. We must help young people see the connection between what they believe biblically and how they live. When we reduce the Bible to a bunch of moralistic stories or a salvation message, we limit the relevancy of God's Word to everyday life. Many families have failed to help young people see Christianity in a holistic and meaningful way.

The gospel has not been as impactful as we had hoped because it is not connected to the broader story of the Bible or the doctrinal truths of Scripture, so when a young person inevitably experiences a trial in life or their beliefs come under attack, their undeveloped faith is no match. That is why biblical worldview is so important. It provides a holistic, robust, deep faith that is centered on the gospel but includes the great doctrines of the Christian faith based on the whole storyline of the Bible.

Families often depend on the church or Christian school to be the primary disciple-maker of their child. Many parents disciple their children by following the model of how they were discipled when they were a child, and that equates to bringing the child to church. According to Lifeway research:

A majority of kids participate in church-related activities but only a fraction develop lasting, personal spiritual disciplines. The reality is that parents are outsourcing more of their children's spiritual development than they may recognize, even if done with the best intentions. ...We can send our kids to Sunday School and Vacation Bible School, but we should not feel that this is enough.[4]

Parents are outsourcing more of a child's spiritual development than they realize. Church-related activities are the primary means that parents use to disciple their children. Consider that 62 percent of parents bring a child to church for Sunday School, small group, or VBS while only 29 percent regularly read the Bible with a child at home.[5]

The church continues to communicate a powerful and unbiblical message to families: Real discipleship happens at church by a paid professional. Families are encouraged to bring a child to the church rather than be equipped to read and discuss the Bible at home and the results have been disastrous.

The discipleship of a young person should include partnership with the church and Christian school, but should not rely on either of these valuable sources as the primary discipling influence. God has designed parents with the role of raising a child to maturity in Christ and it is critical that we operate in obedience to the Lord by joyfully discipling our children.

2. Grandparents

God designed grandparents as the second greatest influence to partner with parents for the discipleship of children. The most concise passage on the role of a grandparent is Deuteronomy 4:9, "Only take care, and keep your soul diligently … teach them to your *children* and *children's children.*"

The Bible has much to say about the role of grandparents. In my book, *Biblical Grandparenting*, I provide an overview of ten biblical themes that summarize the responsibility of grandparents.[6] Each theme speaks to a different component of God's design for grandparents. Together, they present a rich picture of a disciple-making role with a clear task of passing on faith in Jesus Christ to future generations.

TEN BIBLICAL THEMES	
Biblical Theme	Grandparent Responsibility
Grandparents have inherited a faith they are to pass on to their children and children's children (Deut. 6:4–9, 12:28; Ps. 71:16–18).	Build a legacy of faith by passing on biblical teachings, traditions, and faithfulness.
Grandparents are to leave an inheritance to future generations (Prov. 13:22; Eccl. 7:1).	Provide children and grandchildren with a financial inheritance and a name that is worthy of honor.

TEN BIBLICAL THEMES	
Biblical Theme	**Grandparent Responsibility**
Grandchildren are desirable and a crowning glory in life (Ps. 128:6; Prov. 17:6).	Recognize the value of grandchildren. Grandchildren are a gift from God.
Grandparents are to be honored (Ex. 20:12; Prov. 23:22; 1 Tim. 5:18).	Future generations have a responsibility to honor grandparents and care for them in their old age.
Grandparents who live in rebellion to God and do not walk in his ways may influence future generations to follow a similar path (2 Kings 17:41; Ps. 103:17; Deut. 4:40; Ex. 34:6–7).	Live in obedience to God and exhort future generations to do the same while warning them of the consequences of sin. Be a living story worthy of imitation.
Grandparents are to have a multigenerational vision for the salvation and sanctification of the family (Ps. 78:1–8; 2 Tim. 1:5).	Proclaim the gospel, point to Christ, and pray for future generations.
Grandparents are to utilize specific spiritual practices to pass on faith to future generations (Deut. 4:9; Ps. 78:1–8).	Build a godly heritage by teaching the truths of God's Word and retelling the story of God's work.

TEN BIBLICAL THEMES	
Biblical Theme	**Grandparent Responsibility**
Old age, the season of grand-parenthood, increases one's potential contribution to God and others (Gen. 2:15; Ps. 92:14–15; Prov. 6:6–11; Deut. 6:1–2).	Reject the narrative that the purpose of old age is a life of leisure and self-indulgence. Choose instead to serve God and bear fruit until one's dying day.
Grandparents have a respon-sibility to the church, which includes the discipleship of younger men and women (Titus 2:1–6).	Older generations are to train younger generations by pro-viding biblical wisdom, guidance, and instruction.
Old age is a sign of God's favor and something to cele-brate (Ps. 90:9–10; Prov. 14:15).	Reject the cultural view of old age as undesirable, embrace old age, and live intentionally for Christ.

Grandparents have been given a God-ordained role in the family to be a disciple-maker of children and grand-children. Grandchildren need active grandparents who enter the battle for the hearts and minds of the next generation. If you are a grandparent, your best days are not behind, and your influence matters. You are to see yourself like the palm tree of Psalm 92, "The righteous flourish like the palm tree ... They still bear fruit in old age; they are ever full of sap and green, to declare that the Lord is upright; he is my rock, and there is no unrighteousness in him" (Ps. 92:12, 14–15). Old age does not diminish your fruit-bearing capacity, it enhances it.

Society tells grandparents to live an indulgent and independent life, and this unbiblical view must be rejected. Grandparents must reject the cultural message that their job is to spoil grandchildren and be a good role model. Grandparents have been given a much larger role than to pray and play with grandchildren.

Adult children, your parents have a biblical role with your children; therefore, it is wrong for you to block them. You are the gatekeeper, and it is important to open the gate. I know there are complex dynamics within each family, so we must do so with wisdom and discernment. Research suggests that five adults are needed in a child's life to help them mature in faith. God provided six, two parents and four grandparents. If you are not partnering together for the discipleship of children, then this may be the next step for you. Have a conversation, talk about expectations, share desires, and work through relational tensions. Provide ways that your parents can invest spiritually in your children.

If you are looking for additional resources on this topic, I have authored or edited seven books on Christian grandparenting: *Biblical Grandparenting* (Scholarly work for deep readers, leaders, and seminaries; the synthesis of my PhD dissertation); *Grandparenting* (great for individual Bible study, small groups, and classes); *Equipping Grandparents* (how to launch a grandparent ministry); *Long-Distance Grandparenting* (how to disciple a child when you live far away); *Overcoming Grandparenting*

Barriers (what to do when there is emotional, spiritual, or physical distance); *Grandparents Raising Grandchildren* (when a grandparent becomes the parent); and *Discipling Grandchildren* (practical ideas to help you implement Deuteronomy 6).

3. Education

Children will spend approximately 16,000 hours in school between kindergarten and twelfth grade. They will be in school nearly sixty times as much as church. Any area of life that significant needs our attention.

Unfortunately, many pastors avoid the topic of education because they do not want to offend parents. Many parents have not thought deeply about what the Bible says on the topic of education and have not explored what children are learning in school. I will examine the topic of education briefly, but I encourage you to visit Renewanation.org to learn more about what children learn in public schools and the value of Christian education as a partner in the discipleship of children.

A word about education

If you are involved in a public school as a teacher, parent, or grandparent then it will likely impact how you read this section. Know that as I write, I am not condemning you or your decision. I'm writing this section to raise awareness so that education does not destroy your child's faith in Christ. Let me say three things so that this section is helpful for you.

1. My hope is that you will objectively consider what I write on this subject without being unnecessarily influenced by your experience.

2. I want you to see the incredible impact that 16,000 hours has on your child so that if you feel compelled to continue in the public school system, you double your efforts to disciple your family to counter the unbiblical teaching they will receive.

3. If you feel agitated by what you read, please know that I'm not purposefully trying to upset you. I want to encourage you to read to the end and test what you read against the Bible. More than likely, this section will simply introduce you to these ideas and additional study will be needed. If additional study is desired, *Kingdom Education* by Glen Schultz and *Total Truth* by Nancy Pearcey are good places to start.

There are several common forms of education today: public, private, Christian, charter, and homeschools. The real issue is not public vs. Christian or private vs. homeschool. We must address the real issue when it comes to education, which is the philosophy behind the type of schooling. All schools are based on one of two philosophies of education: a secular philosophy or a biblical philosophy.

Secular education ignores or denies the existence of God and teaches a child to develop a secular worldview.

A secular philosophy of education can be the foundation for any of the five types of schools mentioned above. Christian schools and Christian homeschools should be built on a biblical philosophy of education, focus on discipleship, and make it their mission to instill a biblical worldview.

Introduction to Secular Humanism

If your child or grandchild is in a public school, the child is immersed in humanism. Secular humanism is one of the most predominant religions in America. It is taught in every public school, even those in rural communities and those with high numbers of Christians who teach at the school. Secular humanism is present in the goals of education and in the curriculum of every subject, and is absorbed by children. It is critical that you understand what secular humanism is so that you can identify it, train your children to reject the lie, and protect them from error.

- Nancy Pearcey states, "Secularism itself is based on ultimate beliefs, just as much as Christianity is. Some part of creation—usually matter or nature—functions in the role of the divine. So the question is not which view is religious and which is purely rational; the question is which is true and which is false."[7]
- John Dunphy, in *The Humanist* states, "The battle for humankind's future must be waged and won in the public school classroom by teachers who correctly perceive their role as the

proselytizers of a new faith; a religion of humanity."[8]

- Humanist Charles Potter wrote, "Education is thus a most powerful ally of humanism, and every American school is a school of humanism. What can a theistic Sunday School meeting for an hour once a week and teaching only a fraction of the children do to stem the tide of the five-day program of humanistic teaching?"[9]

The effect of secular humanism has been to marginalize God, make the Bible irrelevant to everyday life, and erode faith. Naturalism and relativism have become subtle replacements for the supernatural and absolute truth. Here is a quick overview of the differences between Christianity and secular humanism.

CHRISTIANITY	SECULAR HUMANISM
God exists. He is the center of all things.	God does not exist. Man is the center of all things.
God created the world.	The universe came about by random chance. There is no designer.
God created humans in his image for a purpose. Humans exist to glorify God.	Humans exist for no ultimate purpose other than their own happiness.

CHRISTIANITY	SECULAR HUMANISM
Humanity is totally depraved and has rebelled against a perfect God.	Humanity is good.
Morality comes from God and is revealed in the Bible.	Morality is relative. There is no absolute standard of right and wrong.
Jesus is the way, truth, and life. Salvation comes by faith in Jesus.	Jesus is not God. Humanity has the power to save.
Death ushers us into eternal life or eternal death.	Death is the end of all existence.

Education is never religiously neutral. God has simply been removed from the classroom and replaced with atheism, which has its own set of convictions and beliefs. Theologian Gordon H. Clark observed, "The school system that ignores God teaches its pupils to ignore God, and this is not neutrality. It is the worst form of antagonism, for it judges God to be unimportant and irrelevant in human affairs. This is atheism."[10]

In secular humanistic thinking God becomes weightless and has little bearing on the actual life of a Christian. Young people may not disbelieve in him for salvation, but he is distant in their thinking. They are erroneously trained to believe that the Bible has little to say about science, history, government, economics, or justice. Ultimately, God becomes irrelevant. At best, he is a therapeutic God who emotionally comforts and provides a moral example of how to love others. "Without God," writes David Wells, "all we have left is sentiment."[11] Wells believes that the result is practical atheism that reduces Christianity to nothing more than the services it offers or the good feelings it generates.[12]

Public education has helped to create dualism where the sacred and secular are split into two different spheres. God is relegated to one's private life for pietistic purposes, but has little value in public life. The dichotomy is unbiblical as it rejects the lordship of Christ. The Bible does not present two realms, one that is spiritual and one that is not. Education in the Bible is holistic, predicated on the view that the fields of learning all find their place under the single umbrella of discovering God's truth in God's world. When the Bible is disengaged from learning, a child's views and values become shaped by whatever is the socially accepted status of the day, which is increasingly antithetical to Christianity. The unifying center is no longer biblical truth, and therefore there is no link between learning and God. Children are being taught an incorrect understanding of the world, human life, and God. Public schools are immersing children in secular humanism, and Christians have accepted it with disastrous results.

Humanism elevates man above Christ. Humans become the center of education. In contrast, Ephesians 1:22 states, "[Jesus] put all things under his feet." Colossians 1:18 states "that in all things [Jesus] may have the preeminence." Humanism removes God and substitutes man in his place. Modern-day American public education is no longer about man studying God, but man studying man. Instead of placing faith in God, children are taught to place faith in man. It is around this surrogate center that God and his world are made to spin. When God becomes an awkward appendage to all that children are taught, we are foolish to think that God will have any meaningful place in their lives.

Children are being taught an alternative view of life, one that is not centered on God and his truth. Why should a child see Jesus as Lord of his life when Jesus isn't even viewed as Lord of the world? Why should a young person see God as relevant when he has been treated as another kind of knowledge with a separate set of rules and operating procedures from the rest of life?

The man-centered focus of humanistic education results in a view of life that is driven by self-fulfillment as its overall aim. The highest achievement in public education is self-actualization: the autonomous, independent individual finding meaning and fulfillment in nothing but himself. Young people are encouraged to reject ethics, explore anything that makes them happy, and fulfill their unlimited potential by constructing their own identity.

There is a battle for the hearts and minds of our children and it is being fought in classrooms across the country. Unfortunately, many Christians don't realize this. David Wells summarizes how many parents, grandparents, and pastors operate when it comes to public education:

It is only where assumptions in culture directly and obviously contradict articles of faith that most evangelicals become aroused and rise up to battle 'secular humanism'; aside from these specific matters, they tend to view culture as neutral and harmless. More than that, they often view culture as a partner amenable to being co-opted in the cause of celebrating Christian truth. I cannot share that naiveté; indeed, I consider it dangerous. Culture is laden with values, many of which work to rearrange the substance of faith.[13]

Most parents see the sex-saturation of culture and know there are LGBT messages in education. Parents are aware that evolutionary perspectives exist in textbooks, but beyond these two obvious issues many parents are unaware of the depth and pervasiveness of the unbiblical messages that are taught by teachers and textbooks. The perspective that culture is neutral and harmless is dangerous. Education is one of the most powerful influences that can cause a young person to think in an unbiblical way. Many Christians believe in the religious neutrality of public education and for this reason are exploited by it and taught unbiblical views that destroy faith in Christ and erode trust in the Bible.

Biblical education
Many individuals think that the Bible is silent about education. The Bible never mentions the word education, but

God has much to say about teaching children, and these references help us develop a biblical view of education. Education is the parent's responsibility, so if a child is sent to a public or Christian school, parents still have the responsibility to be actively involved and pay careful attention to what the child is taught and is learning. Biblically, schools are the adjunct servant to the home and this helps a parent understand the role they need to fill educationally.

Education is discipleship. A disciple is a learner whose goal is to become like the teacher. Luke 6:40 (NIV) states, "The student (some translations say disciple) is not above the teacher, but everyone who is fully trained will be like the teacher." By nature, education shapes. It forms a student into the likeness of the teacher, institution, and curriculum. Education is a process of growth involving the church, home, and school. Educating children is deadly serious business, which is why we are reminded that it is better to be drowned with a millstone than to lead a child astray (Matt 18:6). If you are looking for additional information to help you develop a biblical understanding of education then I highly recommend *The Renewanation Review*, a free magazine available at Renewanation.org.

4. Peers

Peer relationships create a gravitational pull toward good or evil. Our aim as parents and grandparents is to encourage our children to develop friendships with Christ at the center, as this is a biblical principle that will encourage good decisions and wise living. "The one who walks with the wise will become wise, but a companion of fools will suffer harm" (Prov. 13:20 csb). The parent or grandparent who ignores this principle and allows a child to develop deep relationships on a foundation other than Christ risks their child suffering harm.

According to the Bible, as well as the Barna study mentioned at the beginning of this chapter, it is not an inconsequential matter who our children befriend. Help your child choose Christian friends. Invite them to your home. Create an environment that encourages friends to come over. It will give you the opportunity to informally spend time with, get to know, and influence the individuals your child chooses as friends.

One of the biggest laments that I hear from parents is that their child did not have a good Christian friend. Be intentional, not passive in this regard. Don't wait for the friendship to find your child. Help your child develop at least one strong friendship in Christ by being actively involved in your local church (you can't develop friendships if your child isn't there regularly), identify strong Christian families or young people, and spend time with these families in an informal way. You can initiate. Get a group of boys together to play flag football, have a campout in your backyard, get the girls together to do nails, or have a Nerf war. Do not rely on your church to find or foster these relationships.

5. The Church

The Bible presents a family-centered, church-supported strategy to disciple children, and this needs to shape *how* we minister to young people. As impactful as churches and Christian schools are, we can't get the job done without parents and grandparents doing what God has called them to do. If we do not understand this critical truth, pastors or educators may unintentionally usurp a role that is not theirs and demotivate the family from active discipleship.

Parents rely heavily on the church for the discipleship of a child, yet ironically, are attending church less often. "The average child attends an evangelical megachurch less than two times per month."[14] Infrequent church attendance has become the norm for families.

Lifeway research found the frequency of church attendance impacts lifelong faith in Christ. They found, "For each drop in frequency of family church service attendance while growing up, a young adult has a corresponding 1.25 percent drop on spiritual health. ... A widespread American trend is having an effect, and our children are paying the price."[15] The author of the study asks, "For parents, we must begin by asking ourselves if those odds are worth the risk when it comes to the future of our children and potential grandchildren. For church leaders, we must begin by asking if we are doing everything within our ministry parameters to educate parents and partner together for the good of the next generation."[16]

Your child's spiritual health and biblical worldview, in part, will be shaped by your involvement in a local church. Here are four applications that you should consider:

- *Choose a Bible-saturated church.* Does the church preach through passages of the Bible and teach sound doctrine? What Bible studies and classes are offered for the congregation? Does the church teach the Bible to children and youth or focus more on entertainment with a short devotional?
- *Make the decision to attend church once and stick to the commitment.* Establish the pattern of weekly worship with a local congregation so that it is not a decision or discussion that happens on a weekly basis. Do not give your child the choice to attend church.
- *Prioritize worship over athletics, academics, and the arts.* Weekly worship should be a non-negotiable on your calendar. Block it off and schedule around it. People do what they value, so a lack of church involvement signifies a low view of the church and misplaced passions. Take a moment and look at your calendar. What gets the first and best of your children's time?
- *Worship together as a family.* Children's worship and youth ministry should never become a replacement for corporate worship. They are not the same thing. What would be the effect on your family and your children if you had a kid table and an adult table for every family meal at your home? What is the effect on

children when we do that very thing for eighteen years at church? The pattern of Scripture is for children to worship with their family.

The combination of limited family discipleship, unbiblical messages in public schools, and infrequent church attendance has become a lethal combination that is distorting, and in many cases destroying, the faith of children raised in Christian homes.

Conclusion

Children become like the people they spend time with. In the book *Lost in Translation*, Dr. Christian Smith offers the following assessment regarding what shapes the spiritual life of young people:

Most of the problems in the lives of youth have their origins in the larger adult world into which the youth are being socialized. It might be the problems of the adults in their immediate lives—their parents, relatives, teachers, family friends and so on. Or it might be the priorities, values, practices, and institutions of the larger adult world they inhabit—schools, mass media, shopping malls, advertising, and the like. But one way or another, adults and the adult world are almost always complicit in the troubles, suffering, and misguided living of youth, if not the direct source of them. The more adults can recognize and admit that fact—the sooner we will be able to address some of the young people's problems more constructively.[17]

Parents, grandparents, educators, and pastors are almost always the direct source regarding what children believe and who they become. We would be wise to assess *who* is shaping our children and *how* we are discipling our own family. The Bible clearly teaches that what we sow today, we reap tomorrow. If we plant our children in the soil of ungodly influences, unbiblical thinking, and non-Christian relationships, then we can expect fruit to grow in accordance with these influences. We must take our family discipleship role seriously and commit to helping children think and live biblically.

PART 2

THE BIBLICAL FOUNDATION

How to Help a Child Develop a Biblical Worldview

How does a child develop a worldview? What can parents and grandparents do to biblically, intentionally, and strategically help a young person develop a biblical worldview?

The Bible is full of methods to raise children to maturity in Christ and to accomplish the task that God has given us to make disciples of future generations. Examples include proclaiming the gospel, communicating wisdom, warning, teaching the Bible, correcting, rebuking, training in righteousness, asking questions, testimony telling, communicating a blessing, intentional meals, prayer, memorizing Scripture, and reading the Bible. Each of these biblical methods are God-designed tools that we should incorporate into family discipleship and worldview training. Because the nature of this book is introductory, space limits my ability to explore each of these biblical methods sufficiently. Rather than address each topic briefly, I'll focus exclusively on the importance and usage of the Bible in helping children develop a worldview.

Every young person will ask three questions about the Bible: Is it true? Does it apply? Will I follow? We must diligently work to answer these questions and persuade a child to embrace the authority and sufficiency of Scripture. This section will help you train a young person to believe the Bible, learn the Bible, and live the Bible.

4

HELPING CHILDREN DEVELOP A LOVE FOR THE BIBLE

BEGINNING WITH A STRONG FOUNDATION

Biblical worldview is built on the foundation of strong doctrinal beliefs about the Bible. A child's views about the Bible will shape the child's views about life. Sound doctrinal beliefs will lead to a strong biblical worldview that results in wise choices and righteous living. Distorted beliefs will lead to foolish decisions and crooked living. An erroneous interpretation of the Bible will result in an erroneous worldview. Therefore, a correct understanding of the Bible is paramount.

What a young person believes *about* the Bible is a matter of utmost importance. A battle exists for the Bible. The world wants to destroy the authority and trustworthiness of the Bible as well as distort its truth in the eyes of our children, which is why we must work diligently to establish its authority, prove its reliability, show its trustworthiness, and apply its usefulness to all of life. This chapter provides a concise overview of key doctrines about the Bible that should be taught to every young person as well as read and discussed together.

Develop a high view of the Bible

It is no light matter what our young people believe and do with the Bible. It concerns the life of their soul. The Bible never becomes obsolete or outdated. It is always green, fresh, and new. It is a well that is never dry, a field that is never barren, and a mine that is never exhausted. It applies to the heart of every person, in every country, at every age and stage, and at every point in history.

The Bible is the Word of God and is to be received with thanksgiving. It is to be believed as God's instructions, obeyed as God's commands, and embraced as God's promises. No other book in history comes near its wisdom, accuracy, and majesty.

Civilization is indebted to the Bible for many of its best institutions. From the Bible are drawn the best laws by which society is kept in order, the standards of marriage, and the roles and responsibilities of every member of the home. To the Bible we owe nearly every humane and charitable institution in existence. The sick, poor, orphaned, or disabled were seldom thought about before the Bible. It is the Word of God that resulted in hospitals and schools.

Had it not been for the Bible we may have lived in chaos and died in misery.

There is a reason the Bible is the best-selling book of all time: It is the only book ever written by God. The Bible explains the origin of life, the purpose of our existence, how we are to live, and what we can expect in the future. If the Bible is unreliable in what it teaches about these things, then we are left to speculate and the Bible is of no value to the world. Without the Bible we would not know the answers to life's main questions. J.C. Ryle, a 19th century pastor, provides six reasons the Bible is valuable:[1]

- *The Bible alone gives the true account of creation.* The Bible informs us that God created the world by speaking it into existence in six days to bring glory to himself.
- *The Bible alone gives a true and faithful account of man.* It does not flatter him as current literature does nor does it conceal man's faults or exaggerate his goodness. It describes man as a fallen creature, inclined to evil and fully corrupt, by nature always a sinner—needing redemption, a new heart, and to be made fit for heaven.
- *The Bible alone gives us true views of God.* Because of the Bible we know God hates sin; the destruction of the world by the flood, the burning of Sodom and Gomorrah, the drowning of Pharaoh and his army in the Red Sea, the overthrow of

Jerusalem, and the scattering of the Jews all are known because of Scripture. We also know that God loves sinners. He provided a wonderful promise at the fall of Adam and Eve, is long-suffering as shown at the time of Noah, delivers Israel out of Egypt, gives the gift of the law, and brings Israel to the Promised Land. God sends prophets to warn Israel, sends his Son into the world, and proclaims the gospel to Gentiles.

- *The Bible alone teaches us that God has made a perfect and complete provision for the salvation of sinful man.* The Bible tells of the sacrificial death of Jesus on the cross for the sins of the world. It tells that Jesus took man's place, became our sacrifice, paid for our sin to obtain redemption for all who believe in him. It tells us that the law has been satisfied and sin has been remedied.

- *The Bible alone explains the state of the world.* There are many things in the world that the non-Christian cannot understand or explain. Poverty, oppression, war, and the existence of evil are puzzling to him. The Bible explains that man is evil and inclined to wickedness. Neither laws nor education can change man's heart. The Bible tells us that a better time is coming with no pain, tears, or death. The Bible tells us to prepare for Christ's second coming.

- *The Bible alone gives an account of the God-man Jesus Christ.* Four separate witnesses tell us of his miracles and ministry; his words and his ways; his life and his death; his power and his love; his perfection and his patience. There is one thing that no reader can fail to grasp and that is the character and work of Jesus Christ.

How instructive are the examples the Bible provides. How precious are the promises the Bible contains. How blessed are the hopes the Bible holds out to the believer in Jesus. How deep is the wisdom contained in its pages. All these things man could find nowhere else except the Bible. Thus, it is no light matter what we are doing with the Bible.

Despite its incomparable worth, a battle for the Bible exists. Is it trustworthy and true? Is it error free? Does it have the authority to dictate right from wrong and to tell humanity how to live? Is it sufficient to tell us all that we need to know in order to parent, teach, pastor, or mature in faith? It is more crucial than ever that young believers understand what the Bible is and why they can trust it wholeheartedly.

Where did the Bible come from?

The Bible came from God; every chapter, every verse, every word is from God. Many versions use the phrase "God-breathed" to tell us it is from his mouth (2 Tim. 3:16). The Holy Spirit is the author. What the Bible says, God says. Its authority is his authority, for he is the ultimate author. God chose and prompted men to write the messages he gave to them. In freedom and faithfulness they "spoke from God as they were carried along by the Holy Spirit" (2 Peter 1:21). The contents of the Bible were communicated to its writers in thoughts, visions, dreams, and at limited times through dictation (the Ten Commandments). The Bible authenticates itself by speaking to its own reliability, and our experience with Scripture confirms it is of divine origin. Ryle states,

> We all know how difficult it is to get a story told by any three persons, not living together, in which there are not some contradictions and discrepancies. If the story is a long one, and involves a large quantity of particulars, unity seems almost impossible among the common run of man. But it is not so with the Bible. Here is a book written by not less than thirty different persons. The writers were men of every rank and class in society. One was a lawgiver. One was a warlike king. One was a peaceful king. One was a physician, another as a learned Pharisee, two as fisherman, several as priests. They lived at different intervals, over a space of 1500 years; and the greater part of them never saw each other face to face. And yet there is a perfect harmony among all these writers. They all write as if they were under one dictation. The handwriting may vary, but the mind that runs through their work is always one and the same. They all tell the same story. They all give one account of man, one account of God, one account of the way of

salvation, one account of the heart. You see truth unfolding under their hands as you go through the volumes of their writings—but you never detect any real contradiction, or contrariety of view.[2]

The Bible is not of man; it is of God. We should read the Bible as if we have heard God audibly speak its message. That is, it carries the same weight of authority as if God himself were speaking its words.

Inspiration not only includes the words that were written, but the books of the Bible that were chosen. The Bible is complete. Nothing should be added to or subtracted from the Bible. The book of Mormon, the Koran, or any other holy book must be rejected as the thoughts of man, not the words of God.

The Bible, no doubt, contains many hard things to understand, or else it would not be the Word of God. It contains things above our reasoning, not because it is false, but because we have limited understanding and God is greater and grander than our mind can ever comprehend. We ask children to believe many things that they cannot understand or see the meaning of, and this is to be true of us with the Bible. We ought to expect to find the "deep things" of God within the pages of the Bible (1 Cor. 2:10 NIV). For those who persevere, the Bible's meaning will be made clear.

Why did God give us the Bible?

Without the Bible, we could only know God in part. Prior to the Bible, we could know God through creation and conscience. Creation proves the existence of God, but tells us little about his character or nature. Our conscience informs us of right and wrong and loudly tells us that we need a Savior. God gave us the Bible to reveal himself to lost humanity through Jesus Christ.

The Bible is God's witness to himself. It shows us the way that leads to heaven. It shows us everything we need to know, everything we need to believe, and everything we need to do. It will show us what we are—sinners. It will show us who God is—perfectly holy. It will show us the great redeemer—Jesus Christ. It will show us how to live—wisdom.

The Bible is the grand instrument by which souls are converted to Jesus Christ. The mighty change is often begun by a text or doctrine of Scripture as it sinks into the heart of man. The Bible is "able to make you wise for salvation through faith in Christ Jesus" (2 Tim. 3:15). God gave us the Bible to make us wise for salvation. God caused the Bible to be "written for our instruction" (Rom. 15:4). No book in existence contains such important content as the Bible. A well-taught Sunday school student knows more truth than a non-Christian with a PhD.

God has declared the Bible is "profitable" for us. It is given for our learning, a sword with which all soldiers of Christ should be armed, and a light to our feet. 2 Timothy 3:16 tells us that the Bible is to be used for teaching, conviction, correction, and training in righteousness. It is the primary way young people are built up and established in their faith. It is the Word of God that causes growth, teaches a person how to walk in this world, and how to live to please God in all matters of life. It teaches us how to be a good son or daughter, husband, wife, father, mother, grandparent, educator, pastor, employee, or neighbor.

It enables us to face suffering and say, "All is well" (2 Kings 4:23; 26). It enables us to look at the grave and say, "I fear no evil." It enables us to look at eternity and not be afraid. It enables us to bear persecution without flinching. Though a person may be alone, if he has the Bible he has the unfailing guide that will teach the road to heaven and way of life.

What is the Bible about?

The Bible was written over a span of 1,500 years by more than thirty authors and contains sixty-six individual books all with the same message. The Bible is not a random collection of writings, but a unified whole.

Whatever portion of the Bible one is studying, it is important to remember that the person and saving work of Jesus Christ is the ultimate focus of Scripture. Jesus himself said, "You study the Scriptures diligently because you think that in them you possess eternal life. These are the very Scriptures that testify about me" (John 5:39 NIV). In addition, Jesus spoke to two disciples on the road to Emmaus and "beginning with Moses and all the Prophets, he explained to them what was said in all the Scriptures concerning himself" (Luke 24:27 NIV).

A helpful way to think about the whole of the Bible is with the phrase *promise and fulfillment*. In the Sermon on the Mount, Jesus said, "Do not think that I have come to abolish the Law or the Prophets; I have not come to abolish them but to fulfill them" (Matt. 5:17). When speaking of the Scriptures, Jesus uses the categories of promise (for the Old Testament) and fulfillment (for the New Testament). The same concept is found in 1 Peter 1:9–12 and Matthew 11:12–13. When reading the Bible, one should ask these basic questions: *Am I reading the promise or fulfillment part of Scripture? In what way is Christ anticipated or fulfilled in this text?*

The Bible is not a random collection of people or events. It is a unified whole with one main storyline pointing to, revolving around, and fulfilled in Jesus. There are four major parts of the Bible: creation (Gen. 1–2), fall (Gen. 3), redemption (Gen. 4–Rev. 20), and restoration (Rev. 21–22). As we read through the Old Testament we can help our children see how it points to Jesus and his covenant of salvation. Jesus was the final Adam (Rom. 5:12–21), the final prophet like Moses (Acts 3:22; 7:37), the final high priest (Heb. 7:23–24), the final Passover sacrifice (1 Cor. 5:7), the final manna from heaven (John 6:31-32), the final suffering servant of Isaiah 53 (Mark 10:45), and the final Son of Man of Daniel 7 (Matt. 24:30). Jesus himself did this, as mentioned above. Noah's ark is about much more than cute animals getting on a boat and Noah obeying. David conquering Goliath is much more than bravery that helps a person overcome giants. Each person, each story, each episode ultimately is in the Bible so that God is glorified and this happens through the salvation and judgment of people.

One of the primary roles of the Holy Spirit is to help us understand the Bible and to see Jesus on every page and in every passage. He opens our eyes, softens our heart, and makes it possible for us to grasp the meaning of the Bible.

Let us remember that it is one thing to *have* a Bible, another thing to *read* it, yet most important to *live* it. I am persuaded that many young people have a Bible, but never read it. It sits on a shelf, a stand, or in a book bag. It collects dust and is in pristine condition. Neglect of the Bible is like disease to the body. Every living thing requires food. Our body needs food to sustain and nourish it. It is equally so with our spiritual life. The only food that will sustain and nourish our soul is the Word of God. Let us not read the Bible as a duty, but as a delight. Pray that God will give us an appetite for his Word and a pleasure in reading it.

There is not a single reasonable excuse for not reading the Bible. Many say they have no time to read it. But if a person makes time to eat, sleep, or be involved in athletics or the arts surely they can make time to read the Word of God, which is of much greater value. Many say it is too difficult to understand. But it is written in such a way that the youngest child can grasp its meaning. It is time that you read your Bible this very day. And we should read the Bible daily (Ps. 119:97). Joshua commanded the people of Israel, "This Book of the Law shall not depart from your mouth, but you shall meditate on it day and night, so that you may be careful to do all that is written in it" (Joshua 1:8).

Errors arise from ignorance of the Bible. There are countless young people who know little about the gospel, the exclusiveness of Christ, the commands of God, or the contents of the Scriptures. Many young people cannot explain its core teachings and have little idea of the meaning of faith, conversion, justification, and sanctification. As a result, false teachings are not identified and indifference to false doctrine reigns.

We must not neglect or abuse the Bible. Man has the unfortunate skill of misusing the Bible, misinterpreting the Bible, and therefore, mistreating the Bible. Let us be "mighty in the Scriptures" (Acts 18:24 NKJV). When we read the Bible, pray that God would help you understand it. Like Samuel you may request of the Lord, "Speak Lord, for your servant hears" (1 Samuel 3:9–10).

We are to read the whole Bible and read it in an orderly way. There are many parts of the Bible that many people never read, but the Bible claims that "All Scripture is … profitable" (2 Tim. 3:16). There are some times that it is good to seek out portions of Scripture, but it is most profitable to have a plan and work through a book, or to read through the entire Bible from beginning to end.

Is the Bible true and trustworthy?

Recognizing the Bible is true and trustworthy is foundational for a believer to submit to its authority. Ultimately, the Bible is without error becomes it comes from God himself. Because God is without error, his Word cannot contain errors. "All your words are true; all your righteous laws are eternal" (Ps. 119:160 NIV). We can trust the Bible because we can trust God. The Bible is without error in all its teaching. Jesus testified that the Bible cannot be broken and devoted his earthly life to fulfilling the Law and the Prophets. Jesus provided an example regarding how one is to approach the Bible; he believed the Bible was true and lived his life according to its words. We would be wise to do the same.

The Bible will never fail us. It will not mislead us. The teachings of the Bible are sure, safe, and the reliable rule and guide in all matters of faith and life. In addition, the Bible is free from all falsehood and mistake. This safeguards the fact that the Bible is true in all that it says. Our job is to believe the Bible, receive its teaching, and submit our lives to it.

If the Bible contains errors, then our knowledge of God may be in error. The domino effect is in play—"false in one, uncertain in all." If we believe there are errors in part, how do we know there are not errors in other areas? Departure from complete trustworthiness of the Bible is a serious error, as it is the bedrock on which all else rests.

Resolve to believe whatever you find in the Bible; whether you like it or not. Beware of the danger of receiving some of what the Bible teaches and rejecting other parts. Are you to be judge of what ought to be in the Bible? Do we know better than God? Settle in your mind that you will receive all and believe all, and that what you cannot understand you will take on trust.

How are we to live?

Those who have placed their faith in Jesus Christ as Lord and Savior are called to live out their relationship by faithfully obeying God's written Word (Matt. 28:20). To stray from Scripture, in faith or action, is disloyal to God and is rebelliousness.

A young person must make the Bible his rule for conduct. He must make its principles his principles. He must walk according to the narrow road and follow where Jesus leads. He ought to walk according to the Word, not his neighbor. Remember that we serve a strict and holy God. It is by the Bible we shall be judged, so let us learn to judge ourselves by it.

The Bible is the only measuring stick that determines the truth and validity of all other claims and teachings. No person or institution has the ability or power to state truth from error and tell us how to live. We must receive nothing and believe nothing that is not according to the Word of God. We must test all religious teachings by one simple test: Does it agree with the Bible? What does the Bible say?

Let us weigh books, opinions, sermons, and teachers in the scales of the Bible and value only that which conforms to the Word of God. The main question: Is it biblical? If it is, it should be received. If not, it should be refused and rejected. If you neglect the Bible, there is no degree of error into which you may not fall.

Conclusion

The Bible must shape what we believe from beginning to end. All true Christians love the Bible. Just as a child naturally desires his mother's milk, so the born-again Christian desires the milk of the Word (1 Peter 1:23; 2:2). It is a common mark of all believers that they "delight in the law of the Lord" (Ps. 1:2 NLT). Let us say with the psalmist, "O how I love your law!" (Ps. 119:97). Love of the Word was a mark of Jesus Christ. He read it publically, quoted it continually, and explained it frequently. He advised people to "search" it (John 5:39). He used it as a weapon to resist the devil. Love of the Word is prominent in the life of Christ and it should be for us as well.

Read the Bible in a spirit of obedience and application. Read the Bible with the determination that you will live by its rules, rest on its statements, and act on its commands. As you read through each chapter ask, "What does this teach me?" and "How am I to live accordingly?" Train your children and grandchildren to do the same.

We are held responsible for what we do with the Bible and the teachings that it contains. James tells us, "Do not merely listen to the word, and so deceive yourselves. Do what it says" (1:22 NIV). May we heed James' advice.

5

UNDERSTANDING THE AUTHORITY OF SCRIPTURE

BUILDING A CASE FOR THE TRUSTWORTHINESS OF THE BIBLE

In every generation there are new and creative attacks on the Bible. The battle for the Bible can occur anywhere—in a conversation with a skeptical peer, a mocking remark on social media, a science textbook at school, or even a Bible course in college

Prominent atheist Professor Richard Rorty admits that he is actively trying to destroy the faith of Christian students in college. He boldly revealed his plans: "We are going to go right on trying to discredit you in the eyes of your children, trying to strip your fundamentalist religious community of dignity, trying to make your views seem silly rather than discussable." He said professors "arrange things so that students who enter as bigoted, homophobic religious fundamentalists will leave college with views more like our own."[1]

The Bible is attacked more than any other book, so we must prepare children with a strong biblical foundation. One way to do that is to build a case for the trustworthiness of the Bible and help young people apply the authority of Scripture to life. The doctrine of authority is based on an important question: How do we know the Bible is the Word of God?

Eight reasons to believe the Bible is the Word of God

1. Self-Authentication. The Bible claims to be the Word of God: "All Scripture is inspired by God" (2 Tim. 3:16 NLT). Jesus, Paul, and other New Testament writers believed the Old Testament was authoritative, they quoted it often, and lived in obedience to it. The witness of Jesus vindicates the authority of the Bible. Jesus believed the Psalms were inspired by the Holy Spirit (Mark 12:35–36). Jesus believed that the laws God communicated to Moses are to be believed and obeyed (Matthew 19:3–6; John 5:46). Jesus believed all Scripture would be fulfilled (Matt. 5:17–18) and cannot be broken (John 10:33–36).

2. Transformation of lives. The Bible changes the lives of murderers, drug addicts, and atheists. The Bible is not a book about how to live a good life or become a good person. It is a book packed with power to transform lives. "The word of God is living and active and sharper than any two-edged sword, and piercing as far as the division of soul and spirit" (Heb. 4:12 NASB). The Bible is the Word of God and it is able to change lives through Jesus Christ.

3. Circulation. The Bible is the best-selling book of all time. No other book compares with the Bible in its circulation. A good book sells 10,000 copies. An incredible book will sell over 100,000 copies. A few books will sell over 1 million copies. The Bible has sold billions of copies. While this fact does not prove the Bible is true, it proves there is something very special about it. The Bible has been translated into more than 2,000 languages and is accessible to more than 90 percent of the world's population. What makes the Bible so desirable by all people, of all ages, in every country, throughout history? Could it be that it is the true Word of God?

4. Unity of Message. The Bible was written by dozens of authors over fifteen hundred years covering hundreds of topics and it does not contradict itself. Consider that Moses was educated in Egypt and Daniel in Babylon; Joshua was a military commander and David a musician, Solomon was a king, Amos a shepherd, Peter a fisherman, Matthew a tax collector, and Luke a doctor. These writers had very different occupations and backgrounds and lived hundreds of years apart, yet their message is unified. The Bible was written on three different continents—Asia, Africa and Europe—and in three different languages: Hebrew, Aramaic, and Greek.[2] The Bible was written for different purposes such as to warn of coming judgment, to convince people that Jesus was the Messiah, and to address problems in the church, yet there is one unified message: God's glory in salvation and judgment. The Bible's central theme is the person and work of Jesus Christ.

If you put all these factors together, it is amazing that with such diversity there is unity. How is that possible? The Bible is not the work of man, it is the Word of God. "No prophecy was ever made by an act of human will, but men moved by the Holy Spirit spoke from God" (2 Peter 1:21 NASB). God, the one true author of the Bible, guided these writers through the whole process.

5. Indestructibility. The Bible has been attacked for centuries. Skeptics have questioned the Bible. Atheists have tried to discredit it. The Bible has undergone more scrutiny than any book. Despite all the attacks, the Bible proves itself to be true again and again. Many who set out to disprove the Bible become converted to Christianity based on the truthfulness they uncover. No book is as accurate as the Bible.

6. Archaeology. The Bible makes historical references to people, places, and events. Many of these are verifiable. Archaeologists have uncovered the city of Jericho with evidence that the walls fell flat, a ring with Pilate's name on it, and David's city. These discoveries confirm the existence of people and places and verify the reliability of the Bible. Not one historical event or person in the Bible has proven false. Nelson Glueck, a renowned Jewish archaeologist, states, "No archaeological discovery has ever controverted a biblical reference."[3] Dr. William Albright, who was not sympathetic to Christianity, and was considered an authority in Middle East archaeology, said this about the Bible:

"There can be no doubt that archaeology has confirmed the substantial historicity of the Old Testament."[4] Archaeology authenticates the historical accuracy of the Bible.

7. Manuscript Evidence. The Bible has more manuscript evidence to support that it is true than any ten pieces of classical literature combined. John Warwick Montgomery believes that "to be skeptical of the resultant text of the New Testament books is to allow all of classical antiquity to slip into obscurity, for no documents of the ancient period are as well attested bibliographically as the New Testament."[5] In other words, if the Bible is not trustworthy then no other ancient documents are either. Bernard Ramm notes how meticulous the Jewish scribes were in preserving the biblical text:

> Jews preserved it like no other manuscript has ever been preserved. With their *massora (parva, magna,* and *finalis)* they kept tabs on every letter, syllable, word and paragraph. They had special classes of men within their culture whose sole duty was to preserve and transmit these documents with practically perfect fidelity—scribes, lawyers, massoretes. Who ever counted the letters and syllables and words of Plato or Aristotle? Cicero or Seneca?[6]

There are more than 25,000 ancient portions of manuscripts of the New Testament in existence today. No other ancient document comes close to that number. *The Iliad* is second, with more than 600 manuscripts, and the first complete text dates from the thirteenth century. By comparison, the first complete text of the New Testament is only dated to about fifty years from the original manuscript. The high number of copies make it possible to reconstruct the original manuscript with complete accuracy. The following

Author	Book	Date Written
Homer	The Iliad	800 B.C.
Herodotus	History	480–425 B.C.
Thucydides	History	460–400 B.C.
Plato		400 B.C.
Demosthenes		300 B.C.
Caesar	Gallic Wars	100–44 B.C.
Livy	History of Rome	59 B.C–A.D. 17
Tacitus	Annals	A.D. 100
Pliny Secundus	Natural History	A.D. 61–113
	New Testament	A.D. 50–100

table presents a compelling reason to trust that the Bible we have today is the Bible that was written thousands of years ago.[7]

   8. *Prophecy.* Fulfilled prophecy is evidence of the divine authority of the Bible. According to Deuteronomy 18,

Earliest Copy	Time Gap	No. of Copies
c. 400 B.C.	c. 400 yrs	643
c A.D. 900	c. 1,350 yrs	8
c. A.D. 900	c. 1,300 yrs	8
c. A.D.900	c. 1,300 yrs	7
c. A.D. 100	c. 1,400 yrs	200
c. A.D. 900	c. 1,000 yrs	10
4th cent. (partial) mostly 10th cent.	c. 4,00 yrs	1 partial
c. A.D. 1100	c. 1,000 yrs	20
c. A.D. 850	c. 750 yrs	7
c. 114 (fragment) c. 200 (books) c. 250 (most of N.T.) c. 325 (complete N.T.)	+ 50 yrs 100 yrs 150 yrs 225 yrs	5,366

a prophet is false if he made predictions that never came true. There are hundreds of events foretold in the Bible that came true. The prophecies in the Bible are specific and accurate. Isaiah 53 provides details of the crucifixion seven hundred years before the birth of Christ. Cyrus, the king of Persia, is referenced by name in Isaiah 44:28, and we are told he will rebuild the temple of Jerusalem. Daniel records the rise and fall of every nation from Persia to Rome (Dan. 7–8). Jesus fulfilled prophecy about the Messiah. He said to the disciples, "Behold, we are going up to Jerusalem, and all things which are written through the prophets about the Son of Man will be accomplished" (Luke 18:31 NASB). Jesus fulfilled prophecy when he cleansed the temple (Mark 11:15–17), began his ministry (Luke 4:16-21), was betrayed (Mark 14:21), abandoned (Mark 14:27), and arrested as a criminal (Luke 22:37).

If the Bible is true, the message of the Bible is the only means of salvation and the only authority for life. What we believe *about* the Bible determines how we use the Bible in everyday life. Building one's life, home, or ministry on any other foundation would be tragic.

What does biblical authority mean?

Every child will look to an authority to determine truth. The authority the child chooses will determine what the child believes and how the child lives. To choose the Bible as authority means that a person believes the Bible has the power to decide what is good and bad, right and wrong, true and false and to direct how he or she lives.

Authority is not a popular concept. We like to have authority, but not to be under authority. Man in his depravity will continue to rebel against the Bible as truth and God as the ultimate authority. The Apostle Paul tells us that rebellion against God and his Word is natural because man is born spiritually dead (Eph. 2:1; Rom. 3:10–18), blind in his understanding (Eph. 4:18), and unable to accept the things of God because they can only be understood spiritually (1 Cor. 2:14). Only redemption by the Holy Spirit making the sinner spiritually alive can change this reality (Eph. 2:4–5). Newness of life results in illumination of the Bible. The new believer can now understand that the Bible is the Word of God (1 John 2:20). Those who do not have God as their Lord will not have his Word as their authority.

Young people often believe the lie that freedom is acquired by being their own authority. Freedom is not found in the absence of authority, rather it is experienced by submitting to God's authority and living within his boundaries. The commandments of God in the Bible are a means of liberation, and the wisdom of the Bible is a path to blessing. Whenever we put happiness before obedience, we will be destined for misery. Those who place themselves under the authority of God's Word will experience joy.

God is the source of all authority. The Bible conveys the absolute authority of God over all his creation. God is the all-powerful creator of all things (Gen. 1–2) and owns the earth (Ps. 24:1). Psalm 62:11 states, "power belongs to God." Jesus said, "All authority in heaven and on earth has been given to me" (Matt. 28:18). The titles

"Lord" and "God Almighty" declare that God has authority over all the earth.

The Bible is our ultimate authority because it is from God. We do not give the Bible its authority. The Bible is authoritative regardless of what we believe about it. We must decide if the Bible will have functional authority in our life or if we will live according to a different authority. The Bible is our authority when we acknowledge it is true, embrace it, submit to it, and walk in obedience to God's Word. The supreme authority of the universe has given us his Word; therefore, it must have authority over us.

Three categories of illegitimate authority

Many Christians claim the Bible is their authority only to choose a different authority by their actions. Christians look to many other sources for authority. Here are three of the most common that I've observed.

1. Science

Secular voices have convinced many Christians that the Bible is unsophisticated, outdated, superstitious, and unscientific. Even Andy Stanley, pastor of North Point Community Church in Georgia, stated, "When religion and science conflict, at the end of the day if you are an honest person, science must win!" Maybe you've heard someone say, "I know what the Bible says, but you can't deny science." In reality, nothing could be more absurd than thinking human ideas are a more reliable source of authority than God's Word in the Bible. Science is servant to Scripture, not the other way around.

Science becomes an illegitimate source when authority is deferred to human experts. What is science? Science means knowledge. Science is a means to learn about the world God created. The Bible is God's book of science. It contains the foundational truth about biology, history, geology, anthropology, and astronomy. The Bible is an infallible science book. When we create and discover, we are using the laws of physics and chemistry that God has put in place. The laws of science exist because God created an orderly world. The Bible is our scientific authority because the Word of God tells us how God created the world and how the world works.

2. Pragmatism

Pragmatism is an approach that determines actions by the results one desires. It first determines what results are preferred, then decides the actions needed to achieve the desired outcome. Without realizing it, we have become answerable to what works: If giving a reward results in a well-behaved child, wonderful, but if not, threats or ignoring negative behavior may be more effective. If teaching the Bible will attract children to our school or church, great, but if not, focusing on academic rigor or entertainment may be a more effective strategy.

Pragmatism becomes an illegitimate source when authority is determined by personal experience. Pragmatism occurs when we look to our personal experience for direction rather than God's Word. Pay attention to the question, *Does it work?* When this phrase becomes the justification for a decision, you know pragmatism is occurring. Ultimately, pragmatism is the result of biblical ignorance or a lack of confidence in the power of Scripture to do what it promises.

For example, let's consider evangelism. When we look to artificial methods to stimulate conversion or manipulate emotions to get to a desired end, we know that pragmatism is at work. God does not need us to make the gospel relevant. There is not a single creative idea that will bring the spiritually dead to life or contribute to a person's salvation. Paul tells us what brings about salvation: "How from childhood you have been acquainted with *the sacred writings*, which are able to make you wise for salvation through faith in Christ Jesus" (2 Tim. 3:15). The Bible is able to bring about salvation because it brings us into contact with Jesus.

3. Man's Word

The Bible is often replaced by man's authority, which can take many forms. I worked with a pastor who always wanted to make decisions by surveying the congregation rather than applying the wisdom of the Bible. Christians often turn to psychology to solve their relational, marital, or emotional problems rather than the provision that God offers in his Word. The church has even attempted to replace God's Word by declaring itself as the ultimate authority.

Historically, there have been times when the Word of God has been placed under the authority of the church with priority given to its creeds, counsels, articles, and tradition. The Roman Catholic Church is founded on this principle. In their view, the Bible is the Word of God because they have decreed it to be so and confirmed this reality in numerous infallible church councils. There is a major problem with this view. Who authorized the church to make this kind of decision? What is its source of authority to do so? The church can affirm the authority of Scripture, but it is not the source of it. Mark 7:8 (NASB) points out what is happening: "Neglecting the commandment of God, you hold to the tradition of men."

Martin Luther argued that the Catholic Church and the pope did not trump Scripture. Luther was brought before the Diet of Worms in April 1521 and was ordered to recant his beliefs about justification as well as ecclesiastical and biblical authority. His reply left no doubt about his source of authority:

Since then Your Majesty and your lordships desire a simple reply, I will answer without horns and without teeth. Unless I am convicted by Scripture and plain reason—I do not accept the authority of popes and councils, for they have contradicted each other—my conscience is captive to the Word of God. I cannot and I will not recant anything, for to go against conscience is neither right nor safe. God help me. Amen.[8]

In a biblical worldview, ultimate authority belongs to God and God alone. The Bible is to be the foundation for every area of life. Like Luther, we are to be captive to the Word of God. Far too many Christians have a diminished confidence in the Bible. Jeremiah 5:30–31 (NASB) states, "An appalling and horrible thing has happened in the land: The prophets prophesy falsely, and the priests rule on their own authority." An appalling and horrible thing has happened in many homes, churches, and schools—man's word has become the authority. The Bible is God's Word of truth that determines how we live, not surveys, psychology, or even the church.

How does the Bible have functional authority in our life?
It is one thing to say the Bible is our authority; it is another to submit to the Bible as our authority. We must come to the settled conviction that the only authority we have comes from the Word of God. Here are four functional ways we show the Bible has authority in our life.

Turn to God's Word for guidance. We must develop the pattern of looking to God's Word for answers and guidance. Psalm 25:4–5 (NIV) can be our prayer: "Show me your ways, Lord, teach me your path. Guide me in your truth and teach me, for you are God my Savior, and my hope is in you all day long."

Test thoughts and ideas with God's Word. We must learn to cultivate the habit of the mind that filters everything through God's Word. Paul exhorts us to "Test everything; hold fast to what is good" (1 Thess. 5:21).

Take every thought captive with the Bible. We must critique arguments from a biblical perspective and discipline our mind not to allow ungodly ideas to take residence. To do that, 2 Corinthians 10:5 (NIV) tells us, "We demolish arguments and every pretension that sets itself up against the knowledge of God, and we take captive every thought to make it obedient to Christ."

Teach the Bible. We must communicate the whole counsel of the Bible to young people. The Apostle Paul gives Titus this assignment, "These things speak and exhort and reprove with all authority. Let no one disregard you" (Titus 2:15 NASB). Titus is given the responsibility to speak with authority, which comes from the Word of God. Our teaching is not to be occupied with object lessons, good suggestions, or pithy axioms, but rather God's Words from the Bible.

Our authority as parents, grandparents, pastors, and educators comes when we teach and preach the Word of God. This is your responsibility. The Bible is to be your content and curriculum. Titus 2:15 gives three methods to teach the Bible: speak, exhort, and reprove. Speak the Bible so a young person hears and understands it. Exhort so that you persuade a young person to believe and apply God's Word. Reprove by holding a young person responsible to obey and submit to the Bible. We do not invent the message. It is our responsibility to deliver it with faithful interpretation and passionate proclamation so that they understand, believe, and obey God's Word.

Jesus is our example. He taught authoritatively. In Mark 11:28, Jesus was confronted by the chief priest, the scribes, and the elders, who were troubled by Jesus' authority and asked him, "By what authority are you doing these things, or who gave you this authority to do them?" Jesus did not quote rabbis, rely upon the latest research, point to his title or educational degrees, or suggest it was his extensive ministry experience or communication skill that gave him authority. Jesus tells the religious leaders, "My teaching is not mine, but his who sent me" (John 7:16).

If I walk into your home, your church, or your school, will I hear the Word of God taught, read, discussed, sung, prayed, and proclaimed? Or will I hear a different authority? Will I find that you turn to God's Word for decisions, or has an illegitimate authority usurped God's Word when you need direction? Is your confidence in God's Word high or low?

The Bible is to be your authority. It was given by God to parents, grandparents, and pastors to instruct children and grandchildren (Deut. 4:9; 6:6–7). The Bible is able to bring every child to saving faith (2 Tim. 3:14–15). Paul wrote that all Scripture is from God and is useful for teaching, conviction, correction, and training in righteousness (2 Tim. 3:16–17). The Bible is to be your authority for parenting, grandparenting, and ministry to children.

6

TRUSTING THE SUFFICIENCY OF SCRIPTURE

LEARNING TO APPLY GOD'S TRUTH TO LIFE

What a young person believes *about* the Bible is critical. How a young person *applies* the Bible to life is our next concern. The ultimate aim for biblical worldview training is right living. We want to see young people live in *obedience* to the Bible as well as *apply* it to life. In short, we are helping children think and live biblically. Thinking biblically means that we begin with the Bible, seeking a Christian understanding of a topic. We ask what the Bible says about gender, marriage, economics, government, or a long list of other topics. Children can be taught to ask the question "What does the Bible say about _____?" Nothing can be understood if our children do not know the Bible, read the Bible, meditate on the Bible, and know how to apply the truths of the Bible. One way that we help our children think and live biblically is by training them to understand the sufficiency of Scripture. The sufficiency of Scripture helps a Christian apply God's truth to life.

Applying the Bible to Life

There is a growing consensus that Christians do not know how to apply the Bible to life and are looking to other sources for guidance on all matters, including parenting and grandparenting.

- The Barna Group: "Although most people own a Bible and know some of its content, our research found that most Americans have little idea how to integrate core biblical principles to form a unified and meaningful response to the challenges and opportunities of life."[1]
- James Montgomery Boice: "Important as [inerrancy] is, I do not think it is the most critical issue about the Bible facing the American church today. The issue I would pinpoint today is the sufficiency of God's Word."[2]
- John MacArthur: "The one doctrine most under attack in the church of our generation is the sufficiency of Scripture. Even people who give lip service to the authority, inspiration, and inerrancy of Scripture sometimes balk at affirming its sufficiency."[3]

The average Christian operates as if something more than the Bible is needed to navigate life, make decisions in today's world, or raise a child. Christians often affirm the authority of the Bible, yet repudiate it when they look to other sources for guidance.

Let me ask you a few questions about how you use the Bible. Where do you turn for parenting priorities, practices, and problem-solving guidance? Is it the Bible or a different source? Does God give us what we need in his Word to disciple a child to maturity in Christ or do we need to look to outside experts such as psychologists and social research to build upon what God has given us in his Word? Is the Bible enough or is the Bible plus something else needed? Are your problems beyond the scope of the Bible? Are your life decisions and the direction you need found in the Bible? When you need help as a parent or grandparent, where do you turn?

How did you answer these questions? More important, how do you utilize the Bible when you need guidance? Do you know the Bible well enough to apply God's truth to life? For our purposes in this book, what source will we use to help children develop a biblical worldview?

In a study of 2,000 parents, Lifeway found that only 14 percent of parents are familiar with what the Bible says about parenting and believe it is useful as a tool. According to the Lifeway study, Christians look to the following sources for parenting advice: 91 percent look to their own experience, 65 percent look to their parents, 62 percent look to their friends, 58 percent look to their spouse, 46 percent look to the Bible, and 43 percent look to the church. The church and the Bible rank lowest on the list.[4] Parents largely depend on their experience or the experience of others for parenting advice.

In Mark 12:24, Jesus states, "Is this not the reason you are wrong, because you know neither the Scriptures nor the power of God?" Error flows from a lack of knowledge and understanding of the Bible. Jesus once said, "Blessed rather are those who hear the word of God and keep it!" (Luke 11:28). We are blessed when we apply God's Word to life. Let's learn how to do that.

What does the sufficiency of Scripture mean?

The Westminster Confession from 1647 defines the sufficiency of Scripture this way: "The whole counsel of God, concerning all things necessary for his own glory, man's salvation, faith, and life is either expressly set down in Scripture, or by good and necessary consequence may be deduced from Scripture: unto which nothing at any time is to be added, whether by new revelations of the Spirit, or traditions of men." The Bible claims that all things necessary for faith and life are explicitly written in Scripture or can be deduced from God's Word.

The Bible teaches its own sufficiency. Paul tells us that God's "grace is *sufficient*" (2 Cor. 12:9, emphasis added). Nothing else is needed for salvation or strength in times of weakness. Peter proclaims, "His divine power has granted to us *all things* that pertain to life and godliness" (2 Peter 1:3, emphasis added). God has given us everything we need for life. The all-sufficient resources God provides are addressed in 2 Corinthians 9:8 (emphasis added): "And God is able to make all grace abound to you, so that having *all sufficiency in all things at all times*, you may abound in every good work." Every good work that God has called you to, he has sufficiently provided "all things at all times" to enable you to accomplish the task. The Bible contains what we need to faithfully parent, grandparent, work in our career, educate a child, pastor, make a good decision, or find a solution to a life problem.

Applying the sufficiency of Scripture

Let's apply the sufficiency of Scripture to parenting and grandparenting. Not only does God define in the Bible *what* a parent and grandparent is to do, but he also describes *how* parents and grandparents are to make disciples and pass on faith to future generations. God doesn't call parents and grandparents to a task without telling us how to accomplish the outcomes he desires.

If the Bible is all that we had, it would be enough to teach us how to parent and grandparent so that children come to faith in Jesus and grow as disciples of Christ. The sufficiency of Scripture means that we don't need extra-biblical sources to figure out how to parent or grandparent. The sufficiency of Scripture doesn't mean we cannot benefit from additional sources outside the Bible, but it does mean that they are secondary and should never be the primary authority or used as a substitute for the Bible.

Does the Bible shape your perspectives and practices on parenting and grandparenting? That's the critical question. Or do you look to other sources? The actions of many Christians reveal that they do not believe the Bible is sufficient to address life issues or answer our greatest needs. John MacArthur summarizes this well:

> Psychologists claim the Bible is too simplistic to help people with complex emotional and psychological issues. In every quarter of the evangelical movement today the Scriptures are being set aside in favor of novel philosophies, scientific theories, experimental behavioral and counseling techniques, political correctness, and other similar fads of modern opinion.[5]

Second Timothy 3:15-17 and Psalm 19 are the two most comprehensive passages on the doctrine of sufficiency in Scripture and will help us understand how the Bible is sufficient and applies to everyday life, such as parenting and grandparenting.

Second Timothy 3:15-17

One of the most helpful passages on the sufficiency of Scripture from the New Testament is 2 Timothy 3:15–17. Paul warned Timothy of the trials he would face in ministry due to the ungodliness of the world and encouraged him to be on guard against false teachers in the church who creep into homes, are imposters of the truth, and seek to deceive others. Paul reminds Timothy that the answer to these problems is the authority and sufficiency of

Scripture, which is able to lead a person to salvation in Christ, grow them into Christlike maturity, guard from false teaching, and provide direction for life decisions.

> But as for you, continue in what you have learned and have firmly believed, knowing from whom you learned it, and how from childhood you have been acquainted with the sacred writings, which are able to make you wise for salvation through faith in Christ Jesus. *All Scripture is breathed out by God and profitable* for teaching, for reproof, for correction, and for training in righteousness, that the man of God may be competent, equipped for every good work (2 Tim. 3:14–17, emphasis added).

Paul says the Bible is profitable, or useful, for four purposes:

1. *Teaching with the Bible. What is true.* The Bible is given for instruction about what is true and false, such as the meaning of manhood and womanhood, marriage, and what is right and wrong. According to the Bible, teaching is not concerned with facts to be learned, but truth to be lived. Jesus said, "Teach them to obey everything that I have commanded you" (Matt. 28:20 NIrv). One reason God has given us the Bible is to teach children what is true. If we want children to have biblical beliefs, we must commit to

reading and discussing the Bible with them. God gave parents and grandparents the Bible to educate a child in truth.

2. *Convicting with the Bible* (for reproof). *When there is sin.* The Bible generates conviction; it makes people aware of what God requires. The Bible exposes sin. Our children are sinful by nature. They lack conformity to God's law, and God has given you the Scriptures to transform the heart of your child. It is God's ways, not ours, that children must obey. The Greek meaning of the word *reproof* is the legal process of being found responsible for a crime. God has given us the Bible to convince our little lawbreakers they have broken God's law and apart from Christ stand condemned. Conviction is important because there will be no repentance or change without it. Our primary objective as parents and grandparents is to nurture a child's conformity to the character of Christ, which requires conviction that the child is not Christlike in certain areas of life. This is where familiarity with Scripture is helpful, so we can minister the Word when needed. God gave you the Bible to be the prosecuting attorney.

3. *Correcting with the Bible. To make right.* The Bible has the power to correct, which literally means to straighten up what is wrong and

reform. It puts a child back on his feet. Parents are to use the Bible to treat spiritual diseases. God has given you, in the Bible, all the tools to address attitudes, actions, thoughts, and motives that do not align with the character of Christ. What parenting challenge are you dealing with? Sibling rivalry, anxiety, depression, discipline methods—all these parenting issues and more are dealt with in Scripture. The Bible is given to you as the means to bring about repentance, confession, and forgiveness. God gave you the Bible to act as the physician to bring healing, health, and hope. Of course, the Bible itself does not do these things, but it is in the pages of Scripture that we come into contact with Jesus, the Great Physician.

4. *Training in righteousness with the Bible. How to live.* The Greek word for *training* means the rearing or raising of a child. It is the same word used in Ephesians 6:4, which is one reason why this passage applies to family discipleship. The Bible is given for the character training of children. We are to use the Bible, similar to the father in Proverbs, to train a child in moral skillfulness. Children need to be taught to apply God's Word to life. The Bible is given to help children make good and godly decisions and to live in a manner that is pleasing to God. The training of a child involves the discipline

of being made to practice something like a musical piece or athletic skill over and over until it is learned. The Bible is useful to train your child or grandchild to live righteously, which is one of the goals in raising our children and grandchildren. Children, like the rest of us, are inclined to develop sinful habits, and the Bible helps us train children to think, act, and live biblically. God gave you the Bible to be the coach and counselor for children.

God has given us the Bible as the tool to raise our children and grandchildren to Christlike maturity. God did not call us to the task of parenting and grandparenting and then expect us to figure out the best way to reach the goal. He gave detailed instructions about how we are to accomplish the mission and he provided us with "all things at all times" so that "you may abound in every good work" of parenting and grandparenting (2 Cor. 9:8).

In 2 Timothy 3:17 we find a very compelling outcome, "that the man of God may be complete, equipped for every good work." Lots of parents wonder if they are doing the right things as a parent and if their child will be ready to launch into adulthood when they leave home. You can be 100 percent confident that your child has what he or she needs to be equipped for *every good work* that God will call your child to if they are taught what is true, convicted of sin, corrected with God's life-giving words, and trained to live in obedience to God.

Psalm 19

Psalm 19 offers one of the most helpful explanations of the sufficiency of Scripture in the Old Testament. The beginning of Psalm 19 speaks about the importance of divine revelation. The first six verses describe God's revelation in nature, what is known as general revelation. God reveals general truths about himself in creation. Romans 1:20 summarizes this biblical concept, "For his invisible attributes, namely, his eternal power and divine nature, have been clearly perceived, every since the creation of the world, in the things that have been made."

General revelation communicates that God exists and teaches us about a few of God's attributes such as his power and wisdom. However, creation does not reveal anything about salvation or God's moral qualities such as his goodness, grace, justice, or love. God's glory is so great in creation that it should lead every human being on earth to believe in his existence and worship him. The human body, a flower petal, a blade of grass, the complexity of the brain, the nature of light, and the existence of gravity all shout that a Creator was needed for existence.

Paul states that God is "plain" to us, which means that God's existence is self-evident and doesn't require extensive research (Rom. 1:19). Although it is plain, humans suppress the truth and that is why we need God's written revelation in the Bible. Paul tells us in Romans 1:18 that we naturally suppress the truth of God's general revelation by denying his existence or worshiping a false god in his place.

Psalm 19 teaches that there is no conflict between science as found in natural revelation and the Bible. Science and the Bible say the same thing. Harry Ironside wrote, "There is no conflict whatever between the testimony of nature and the testimony of the Word of God."[6] The world God created agrees with the Word God communicated. Those who suggest science and the Bible are in conflict either misunderstand nature or misinterpret the Bible. Charles Spurgeon said, "He is wisest who reads both the world-book and the Word-book as two volumes of the same work, and feels concerning them, 'My Father wrote them both.'"[7]

Psalm 19 was written to elevate the all-sufficient written Word of God over creation. The apostle Peter writes that there is an even greater witness to the truth: "We have something more sure, the word, to which you will do well to pay attention" (2 Peter 1:19).

The second half of Psalm 19, verses 7–11, introduces us to the sufficiency of Scripture as the only trustworthy guidance for life. Take a moment and read verses 7–9:

The Law of the Lord is perfect,
reviving the soul;
the testimony of the Lord is sure,
making wise the simple;
the precepts of the Lord are right,
rejoicing the heart;
the commandment of the Lord is pure,
enlightening the eyes;

the fear of the Lord is clean,
enduring forever;
the rules of the Lord are true,
and righteous altogether.

These verses contain a comprehensive and clear explanation of the sufficiency of Scripture. They speak to the nature and function of Scripture. The psalmist helps us understand what the Bible is and what it does using a form of Hebrew parallelism in which he describes the Bible in six terms: law, statutes, precepts, commands, fear, and ordinances. In the Bible, God communicates truth to humanity concerning what we should believe, the kind of character we should develop, and how we are to live. The Bible is God's teaching for every area of life. These six terms describe the richness of the Bible. The Bible is sufficient for life in six ways:

1. *Scripture is perfect, restoring the soul.* The Bible is perfect; it is not deficient in any way. It is not like the flawed reasoning of humanity. The Hebrew word for *perfect* means complete or whole. It is complete in a way that addresses every aspect of our spiritual life. It is an expression of comprehensiveness that declares the Bible lacks nothing. The psalmist is contrasting the perfection of the Bible with the imperfect and flawed reasoning of men. The word *restore* means to convert, transform,

or refresh. The Bible is so comprehensive that there is no sin or problem the Bible cannot handle. The Bible can deal with all forms of rebellion and is able to convert any sinful heart and transform every area of our life. The Bible is sufficient to convert the soul.

2. *Scripture is trustworthy, making the simple wise.* The Bible is trustworthy or sure. If we follow the practices and principles of the Bible we will not be led astray. We will find salvation, joy, and happiness. Those who base their life on the Bible do not need to be unsure, uncertain, or lack confidence. The truth of the Bible provides an immovable foundation that can be trusted. The biblical word for *simple* presents the picture of an open door. A simple person is like an open door that allows every idea to come in. Such an individual is "open-minded" and doesn't know to shut his mind to false teaching. He is undiscerning and ignorant, but God's Word makes him wise. The Bible is able to provide direction for life decisions. To be wise is to apply the truths and teachings of the Bible to life situations. Wisdom is learning to be skilled in godly living. The Bible is sufficient to be trusted for all your life decisions and directions. There is no life issue that exists outside of what the Bible addresses. The person who thinks he is wise and looks for

instruction outside of the Bible shows he is a fool. In 1 Corinthians, Paul states, "Where is the wise man? Where is the scholar? Where is the philosopher of this age? Has not God made foolish the wisdom of the world? (1 Cor. 1:20). The Bible is sufficient to help us make godly decisions and instruction.

3. *Scripture is right, causing joy.* The word *right* means straight rather than crooked and is connected to righteousness. The psalmist is telling us that it is the Bible that teaches us to walk in a straight path and the result is true joy. The Bible provides all the guidance we need to make good, godly decisions as well as guide us to live in a manner that is pleasing to the Lord. Those who follow the teachings of the Bible are not left to wander around, confused by human opinion. The Bible is sufficient to train us to walk in obedience to God. The Bible is sufficient to give us life direction and guide us in right living.

4. *Scripture is pure, enlightening the eyes.* The Bible gives off light that makes vision possible. The Bible illuminates the right path, which enables us to walk without stumbling in the dark. The Bible makes things clear; it is not confusing or mystifying so we can see clearly, without distortion. The Bible shines light on darkness so we can have clarity and

understanding. The well-known portion of Psalm 119:105 makes a similar point, "Your word is a lamp to my feet and a light to my path." This truth is in contrast with the fog of confusion from unsaved men, who themselves are blind and unable to discern truth or live righteously. God's Word is sufficient to reveal truth and to help us understand it.

5. *Scripture is clean, enduring forever.* God's Word endures because it is pure. The Bible is without any defect, deficiency, error, or shortcoming. Jesus said, "Heaven and earth will pass away, but my words will never pass away" (Matt. 24:35). Biblical truth is flawless and eternal. It never changes. The Bible is never outdated and does not need to be updated, for it is God's revelation for every generation. It is certain, absolute, and grounded in the character of God. A wise person will build her life on the Word of God. The implied contrast is with the corrupt ideas of the world that are rotten and decay. The sufficiency of the Bible means that it never changes, is perfectly applicable, and is always relevant to our needs.

6. *Scripture is true, and righteous altogether.* The Bible warns us against sin and protects us from the lies and errors we will be exposed to. We need the warning of the Bible because error is subtle and pervasive. The Bible is the

means God has given us to stand against deception. The Bible is God's standard for testing the words, fruit, and life of every person. Not only does the Bible warn us of evil and guard us from sin, but it also produces righteousness in those who accept God's Word. The psalmist says that in keeping the laws of the Bible there is great reward. Sin is its own punishment, and obedience is our reward. We are blessed in our obedience. The sufficiency of the Bible means that it corrects us and makes us righteous.

The Bible is God's means to regenerate the lost, is God's cleansing agent for sin, and is God's method to grow followers into Christlike maturity. God has revealed himself generally in creation so that every person is without excuse, yet the only place we can find saving revelation and the only way we can know about Jesus is in the Bible. Without God's Word we will never live a holy life, and children will never develop a biblical worldview.

Far too many Christians have a low view of the Bible and do not know how to use it in everyday life. Second Timothy 3:15–17 and Psalm 19 show us that God gave us the Bible for many uses. Contrary to what is suggested by the actions of many Christians today, there is no need for additional visions or new prophecy. The Bible is able to provide the direction, wisdom, and truth we need for life. Christians need to study and obey what we already have.

Do you use the Bible for the purposes described in 2 Timothy 3:15–17 and Psalm 19, or have you pursued worldly sources in place of the Bible? Many Christians claim to be Bible-based and believe in the truthfulness of the Bible, but do not believe the Bible is sufficient to meet the needs of life for parenting or grandparenting. There has been an abandonment of the Bible in favor of other sources. We must not be people who look to the Bible *and* the world, but to the Bible *alone*.

Psalm 19 concludes with this verse, "Let the words of my mouth and the meditation of my heart be acceptable in your sight, O Lord, my rock and my redeemer" (v. 14). David wanted God to make his words and thoughts biblical. If we want a child to think and live biblically, then we must learn to apply the Bible to life and use it for the purposes that God gave it to us.

The sufficiency of Scripture helps a young person live a biblical worldview. The Bible is useful and profitable for all we need. Will you take God at his Word and trust him to provide what you need? The Bible is true, it is reliable, and it is sufficient to guide us in developing a biblical worldview. Let us look to the Bible to disciple young people with a biblical worldview.

7

SIX WAYS TO HELP CHILDREN LIVE ACCORDING TO GOD'S WORD

TRAINING CHILDREN TO READ AND STUDY GOD'S WORD

Bible-centered living is supremely important in the life of our children. Parents, grandparents, pastors, and educators have the responsibility to teach children to love God's Word and live according to it. Most parents teach children to play baseball, ride a bike, maintain an automobile, and manage money, yet few parents train children to daily read and meditate on God's Word.

As a pastor, I encountered large numbers of Christians, including children, who had never been taught how to have a quiet time and do not read the Bible. As a result, biblical illiteracy is high, moral relativism is common, and doctrinal confusion is widespread. Children cannot live according to God's ways if they do not know God's words.

The Bible encourages us to daily "meditate" on God's Word (Ps 1:2) and to hide it in our heart (Ps. 119:11). These commands apply to adults and children. If you want to significantly influence the faith of children, then make it a priority to teach them to study and memorize the Bible. It is a great gift to give a child a love for God's Word. It is a lasting heritage to train a child to develop the spiritual habit of Scripture reading (Ps. 119:111).

The importance of reading the Bible

What helps children develop deep and lasting faith in Christ? According to a Lifeway study of 2,000 Protestant parents, the following items made the greatest impact on their faith as a child:

1. Child regularly read their Bible while growing up.
2. Child regularly spent time in prayer while growing up.
3. Child regularly served in church while growing up.
4. Child listened primarily to Christian music.
5. Child participated in church missions trips/projects.
6. Child's best friend was an influence to follow Christ while growing up.

7. Child connected with several adults who intentionally invested in them.
8. Parents pointed out biblical principles in everyday life and asked forgiveness when they messed up.
9. Each additional sibling.
10. Child frequently attended church services growing up.[1]

Many parents and grandparents wonder if they are doing the right things and having the right conversations. What we need are not new and novel methods, but a commitment to implement what the Bible calls us to do in the evangelism and discipleship of children. Does it surprise you that this study found the most important things are spiritual habits, serving, media that honors Christ, Christian relationships (friends, family, and education), family discipleship, and church involvement?

According to this study, the greatest impact in the discipleship of children is helping them develop the habit of reading the Bible. All biblical worldview is based on the knowledge of the truth (1 Tim. 2:4; 2 Tim. 2:25; Titus 1:1). The top item on the list reminds us that a biblical worldview is developed, in part, by reading the Bible and meditating on it daily. The more the Bible is read, the more it can be understood and applied to life. It's hard to detect false doctrine and erroneous views when biblical ambiguity exists.

The habit of reading the Bible has not been developed by the average Christian and that is a problem. Lifeway surveyed 2,930 Protestants and found that only 19 percent of Christians read the Bible daily.[2] This means that only 1 out of every 5 Christians who walk into church are reading the Bible. According to a joint study by Barna and Summit ministries, only 17 percent of Christians have a biblical worldview.[3] Is it a coincidence that those two numbers are almost identical?

If you are looking for a high-impact, significant return on investment with children, then train them to read the Bible. Many children have never been taught how to have a quiet time, interpret Scripture, or apply the principles of the Bible to life. Of course, the act of reading the Bible is valuable because of what is in the pages. We don't want our children just to read the Bible. The devil knows the Bible by heart. He used it against Jesus. We want our children to linger in God's Word, to love the truth, to meditate on it day and night, and to plead with the Lord to open their eyes to his beauty.

The Problem of Biblical Illiteracy

Biblical illiteracy is a major problem for young Christians. Woodrow Kroll calls biblical illiteracy an epidemic in America. He suggests that more than 80 percent of Christians of all ages are biblically illiterate, which means that only 2 out of every 10 Christians know how to articulate and defend their faith.[4]

Kroll suggests that biblical illiteracy is lack of familiarity with the Bible, lost knowledge of biblical texts and an inability to correctly interpret them due to the choice to neglect the Bible.[5] Biblical illiteracy is a result of choosing not to read the Bible, and the results are catastrophic. George Gallup Jr. says, "Clearly there is a need to treat biblical illiteracy in this country with all the urgency of a medical emergency."[6] Alex McFarland states,

> The majority of millennials are biblically illiterate. Most of them have neglected reading and applying the Bible. So, of course, when a competing belief or religion comes their way, millennials are unable to defend the Christian faith. One way Satan has been able to do this is through the false teaching of naturalism—an ideology that teaches there is no God, absolute truth, meaning, or afterlife.[7]

If the next generation is going to think and live biblically, grow to be mature Christians, be lifelong followers of Jesus, and impact the world for him, then we have to train them to develop the habit of reading Scripture, properly interpreting it, and applying it to their life. Following are six ways to make that happen.

1. Develop the habit of reading the Bible

Your first priority is to spend time daily reading and marinating in God's Word. "These commandments that I give you today are to be *on your hearts*. Impress them *on your children*," (Deut. 6:6–7, emphasis added). God's progression in this passage is important. God's Word is to be on your heart and then it can be taught to children.

Empty vessels have nothing to give. You cannot pass on to children what you do not have. You will not pass on a passion for Scripture if you do not treasure it yourself. You cannot train children to develop the skills to study God's Word if you have not cultivated it in your own life. If you are a pastor or Christian educator, make sure that doing God's work does not inhibit your time in God's Word. If you are not spending time daily in God's Word, then this needs to be your highest priority.

The joyful experience of reading the Bible is where great parenting and teaching begins. Open God's Word and be blessed by truth and beauty, get captured by its depths and heights, and be captivated by the glorious God in its pages.

2. Practice family worship

Family worship is the means of introducing children to the truths of Scripture and preparing them for the Christian life. The practice consists of reading Scripture as a family, prayer, and praise to God, often through music. God has given the father the role of spiritual leader, but both mother and father are to share in the biblical instruction of children (Eph. 6:4; Prov. 1:8).

The majority of parents do not read the Bible regularly in the home and, as a result, increase the difficulty of raising children in the Lord. Churches and Christian schools can serve families by equipping parents and grandparents to develop the habit of reading Scripture to children and discussing its meaning.

Consider a few practical thoughts:

- *Read the Bible, not someone's thoughts about the Bible.* Devotionals are helpful, but the primary source should be the Bible. My wife and I prioritize the reading of the Bible to our children. We choose passages strategically, based on what we are teaching them. Proverbs is the one book of the Bible written to young people and it should receive heavy emphasis in your home or classroom.
- *Read the entire Bible to children.* The pattern of Scripture is to teach children the deep truths of Scripture. Children were not excused when difficult topics were covered in the Colossian or Ephesian churches. Children were present to be told to obey parents and therefore were taught everything contained in these two books.
- *Read briefly.* Remember, they are children. The younger a child is, the shorter their attention span will be. Don't expect your child to study the Bible like an adult. Try to keep your family reading concise and to the point, but meaningful. Ten minutes is a good amount of time to begin. As children become more comfortable with this spiritual habit, you can increase your time reading the Bible together.

- *Include children in reading and discussion.* Your goal is to explain the Bible passage clearly and biblically, engage children in the process, and help them apply God's truth to life.

If family worship is not a normal habit in your home, do not be discouraged by the child who complains, does not answer questions, or tries to derail the time. Once the child learns that you are serious about reading the Bible on a regular basis, they will get into the routine of listening and responding.

3. Teach children core doctrines of Christianity

Young people are unlikely to remain faithful to a faith they do not understand and cannot defend. Parents and grandparents should teach children of all ages the core doctrines of the Christian faith with a zeal and consistency that follow the pattern of the Bible. As I mentioned previously, we read of Timothy, "*From childhood* you have been acquainted with the sacred writing, which are able to make you wise for salvation through faith in Jesus Christ" (2 Tim. 3:15, emphasis added). And in Psalms we find, "*Since my youth*, O God, you have taught me, and to this day I declare your marvelous deeds" (Ps. 71:17 NIV, emphasis added).

The pattern of Scripture is for children of all ages to be taught the core truths of the Bible so that they will be firmly rooted in Christ and established in their faith (Col. 2:7). The Bible clearly states what will happen to children when they are not well grounded in God's Word.

Here are three examples:

1. Children are taken captive by man's ideas and deceived by human traditions (Col. 2:8).
2. Children become rebellious and live a godless, unfaithful life (Ps. 78:8).
3. Children grow up not knowing God or his great works (Judg. 2:10).

The following topics should be taught to children of all ages:

The Gospel

The gospel is the good news because it addresses our most serious problem. The gospel summarized: We have rebelled against a holy God who created us. God acted in Jesus to save us, and we take hold of that salvation by repentance of sin through faith in Jesus. Concerning the gospel, you should have a threefold aim that your children: (1) clearly understand it, (2) concisely explain it, and (3) confidently proclaim it. A child must personally repent and believe in Jesus Christ.

The Big Picture of the Bible

The Bible is not a random collection of people or events. It is a unified whole with one main storyline pointing to, revolving around, and fulfilled in Jesus. There are four major parts of the Bible: creation (Gen. 1–2), fall (Gen. 3), salvation (Gen. 4–Rev. 20), and restoration (Rev. 21–22).

As you read through the Old Testament, help children to see how it points to Jesus and his covenant of salvation. Jesus himself did this, "And beginning with Moses and with all the prophets, he explained to them the things concerning himself in all the Scriptures" (Luke 24:27 NASB). Jesus is the focus of the entire Bible. The main purpose of reading the Bible is to know more about Jesus so that we become like him.

The primary aim of the Bible is to glorify God and this happens in salvation and judgment found on every page of the Bible. The Bible is about the King and his Kingdom, a theme that runs from cover to cover in Scripture. Read and reread the stories of the Bible to your children with this in mind. Familiarize them with the main stories, people, and events of the Bible, but not in a way that detaches them from the overall storyline of Scripture. We should call our children to obedience to Jesus Christ and can use the heroes of the faith as models to imitate, but let our teaching not dissolve into moralistic instruction separated from the gospel of Jesus or the glory of God.

Doctrine

Doctrine is simply a word to describe what the Bible teaches. Paul challenges young Timothy to "watch your life and your doctrine closely" (1 Tim. 4:16). Every child needs to understand the core doctrines of the Christian faith to grow into a man or woman with convictions to follow God.

The two most critical doctrines for children to learn center on the Word of God and the Son of God. It is a mark of successful parenting to teach children the inerrancy, authority, and sufficiency of the Bible. Great homes train children to embrace the supremacy, exclusivity, deity, and lordship of Jesus Christ. A high percentage of attacks on a child's faith will focus on undermining, destroying, or minimizing their biblical belief in the Word of God and the Son of God.

In addition, we must repeatedly, with greater depth as children age, teach topics such as creation to counter evolution, God's design for marriage between one man and one woman to counter homosexuality, the reality of heaven and hell to counter the claim that death is the end of all existence, the atoning work of Jesus to counter the claim that all religions lead to the same God, the Trinity, and the character of God, to name a few.

4. Give your child a Bible

When my mother was dying of ALS she asked me what I wanted of her possessions to remember her by. My mom had expensive jewelry, money, and things with worldly value, but the thing I wanted most was her Bible. My mom's Bible is the physical expression of the greatest gift that she ever gave me: a love for God's Word. Her Bible is tattered and torn. Its pages are yellow and marked up. It was well used and well loved. I want you to give this same gift to your children.

Purchase a high-quality leather Bible and personalize it for each child. Choose a full-text, readable version that a child can use as they grow older. A good age to give this to a child is during their elementary years, between ages 10 and 12.

Plan a special ceremony or meal around this event. Before giving the Bible to your child, underline or highlight passages you want to emphasize. Make notations in the margins, and write short notes of encouragement and affirmation. May your gift help your child love God's Word and echo the psalmist, "How sweet are your words to my taste, sweeter than honey" (Ps. 119:103).

5. Teach children how to study the Bible

During the early years of a child's life, the parent is the one to feed the child spiritually. But gradually this responsibility should be shifted to the child. For this to happen, parents must teach their child how to read the Bible. Children should be taught basic Bible study methods, which include observation, interpretation, and application. This is known as inductive Bible study.

Observation: We ask the question, *What does this passage say?* Observation is taking a close look at what is going on in the passage of Scripture. Correct observations are key to understanding the meaning of the text. We need to read the Bible thoroughly, slowly, and prayerfully to understand what God is saying.

Interpretation: We ask the question, *What does this mean?* Interpretation is trying to understand the intent of the author. Interpretation is affected by the culture in which the author wrote, the biases we bring to the text, and the context in which the passage is found. We cannot understand a verse without understanding a chapter. We cannot understand a chapter without understanding the entire book. We should teach children to interpret Scripture with Scripture and to consult resources such as commentaries to best understand a passage. Questions that help us understand a passage include: What is good about God in this passage? What is rotten about humanity or needs to be repaired in the world? What is taught about Jesus?

Application: We ask the questions, *What does this passage require of me?* and *What wisdom is taught that can be applied to life?* We come to the Bible for transformation, not simply information. God's Word has the authority to tell us how to live. We train children to obey all God's commands, not just the ones they like. Teach children that obedience is essential, not optional.

6. Provide Bible study tools for children

Every child should understand how to use the following Bible study tools, which make great gifts. Consider building a reference library for each child of the following items:

Commentaries: A commentary simply explains the meaning and application of Scripture. Scholars spend great amounts of time studying the Bible. They write about their discoveries in commentaries. Scripture can be difficult to understand, so good commentaries are helpful for a young person to have.

Bible Dictionary: A Bible dictionary lists items by theme. Using this tool, young people will be taught to look up people, places, and themes of Scripture. Bible dictionaries help a person quickly learn about important and obscure people of the Bible or the meaning of a word. Children can also look up themes such as faith and learn more about the topic.

Concordance: A concordance is a catalog of the Bible. It lists every word by alphabetical order and tells where to find each word by listing references. It is extremely helpful if a young person wants to study a specific word or remembers a word in a passage but cannot remember the reference.

Bible Atlas: A Bible atlas will teach about the geography of the Bible, the location of cities, and the whereabouts of important happenings. For example, there is an Old Testament Jericho and a New Testament Jericho. This is helpful to understand. The Scripture writers purposefully write that Jesus walked up to a location. This is a geographical reference. It is helpful to know where a city is located to better understand a text.

Our aim should be to raise children who are mighty in the Scriptures just like the Bereans: "Now these Jews were more noble than those in Thessalonica; they received the word with all eagerness, examining the Scriptures daily to see if these things were so" (Acts 17:11).

8

HOW TO HELP
A CHILD DEVELOP
A BIBLICAL
WORLDVIEW

UTILIZING COLOSSIANS 2

We must work diligently to convince a child that the Bible is true, trustworthy, and is the authority on all matters of life. Young people also must be trained to embrace the sufficiency of Scripture and learn to apply God's principles and practices to life. After a child trusts in Jesus for salvation, God gives us the responsibility to help the young person mature in Christlikeness (Col. 1:28–29). Central to maturity in Christ is training a young person to think and live biblically. Our goal is a biblical perspective on all of life. One of the most important ways to do this is to help a young person read the Bible, because in its pages the young person will hear from God, receive direction for life, and be transformed into Christ's image.

Paul presents a two-step process in Colossians 2:6–8 that we can use to help children develop a biblical worldview. The first step is to teach children biblical truth so that they receive Christ, walk in his way, and become deeply rooted in the faith (Col. 2:6–7). Paul wants believers to be built up in Christ and to establish lifelong faith. How does this happen? Paul tells us, "just as you were *taught*" (Col. 2:7, emphasis added). There is a correlation to teaching biblical truth and lifelong faith in Christ.

Core Biblical Truths

The entire Bible needs to be taught to children, but there are key doctrines and core truths that should receive greater emphasis in our teaching. This list is not meant to be comprehensive, but to provide a manageable number of core truths that should receive prominence in discussion with children and teaching in classrooms. My wife, Jen, and I keep these in mind as we read through the Bible with our children so we can be intentional in shaping the mind and heart of our children in these areas. We also focus on one truth for a season with a specific child to encourage spiritual growth. Write the name of each child or grandchild next to a numbered item and focus on that topic for a season through study of Scripture, discussion, or working through a Bible-based book together on the topic. Over time, move on to another topic. By doing this you will address some of the most important core truths of Scripture with a child.

Bible Theme	Key Bible Verse	Key Idea
The Bible	Tim. 3:15; Ps. 119:160	Is the Bible true? Will I follow it? Biblical authority, inerrancy, and sufficiency. The Bible is the source of truth.
Belief in God	Gen. 1:1	Who is God? Teach a child that God exists. We are to learn about his character and worship him.
Understanding humanity	Gen. 1:26	Who am I? Image of God— what does it mean to be human? We have value and dignity because we are created by God. We are the masterpiece of God's creation. We are not God.
Manhood and womanhood	Gen. 1:27	What is a man or woman? How are they different? What is their role? Celebrate God's good design of male and female.

Bible Theme	Key Bible Verse	Key Idea
Meaning of life	Gen. 1:28	Why do I exist? We exist for a purpose. Focus on the creation mandate, which teaches us to be fruitful and multiply and have dominion. God created us to be his representatives and carry on his work on earth.
Marriage and singleness	Gen. 2:22, 24	What is marriage? What is its purpose? Marriage is one man, one woman, for life. Biblical roles are head (man) and helpmate (woman).
Obedience/ authority/ morality	Exod. 20, Deut. 5, Matt. 22: 36–40; Eph. 6:1–2	What is right and wrong? Key areas of training include: Obey God and fear the Lord. Children obey your parents in the Lord. Respect and submission. Great commandment: Love God, love others.
Sexuality	Song of Songs; Ps. 119:9; 1 Cor. 6:20	What is the purpose of sex? How can a young person stay pure? Rejoice in the wife of your youth. Flee from immorality.

Bible Theme	Key Bible Verse	Key Idea
Suffering	2 Cor. 4:17; 1 Peter 1:6-7, Rev. 21:4	Why do bad things happen? Key subjects include: We live in a fallen world. God is our rock, refuge, and strength in time of need. He is sovereign and works out all things for good. God will make all things new.
Gospel/Jesus	John 3:16; Rom. 10:9	Who is Jesus? What is the gospel? Education begins with salvation. Encourage a child to follow Jesus.
Work/rest/ life skills	1 Cor. 10:31	What is the purpose of work? How should I spend my life? Work to the glory of God. Address laziness, responsibility, and self-discipline. We are saved from something and saved for something.
Wise choices based on godly character	The book of Proverbs	How do I apply God's truth to life? How do I live in a manner worthy of the gospel? Fear God, not man.
Identity in Christ	Ephesians	Who am I? From an object of wrath to new creation.

Bible Theme	Key Bible Verse	Key Idea
Relationship Skills	Col. 3:12–14; 1 Cor. 13, Phil. 2:3–4	How do I love well? Teach children compassion, forgiveness, servanthood, and humility. The Fruit of the Spirit.
Spiritual maturity/ spiritual habits	Josh. 1:8; Matt. 6:9–13; 1 Tim. 4:7	What is the goal? Maturity in Christ (Col. 1:28–29). How do we attain that? (1) Spiritual habits— train yourself to be godly. Study the Bible and prayer. (2) Multigenerational mentoring (Titus 2). (3) Worship and fellowship with believers (Heb. 10:25).
Stewardship of time/ treasure/ talents	Matt. 6:33, Luke 16:13	Everything belongs to God. I am a manager, not an owner. Biblical view of money. Live for eternity. We are sojourners and ambassadors. What does a man profit to gain the world? (Mark 8:36).
Serving/ spiritual gifts	Rom. 12:6–8; 1 Cor. 12:8–10	How has God gifted you? He is King, we are his servants. To live is Christ, to die is gain (Phil. 1:21).

Bible Theme	Key Bible Verse	Key Idea
Make disciples	Ps. 127:3–5; Matt. 28: 1–20	Train them to make disciples. The goal is to see your child develop a lifelong faith so that your child can impact the world for Christ. The Great Commission: Go and grow.

Counterfeit Arguments

The second step to help a young person develop a biblical worldview is to put the best counterfeit arguments in front of them and dismantle them. Show children why that viewpoint is wrong. Many families explain the gospel, but do not provide challenging viewpoints taught in culture and classrooms that contradict the Bible.

In Colossians 2 Paul's emphasis is on danger. He warns believers of false teachings that can be disastrous for one's relationship with Jesus. The spiritual life has its dangers and they come in the form of unbiblical opinions and ideas.

Paul does not want Christians to be taken captive by deceitful ideas (Col. 2:8). The word *captive* means plunder. It is the same idea of being kidnapped. Just as parents warn their children to watch out for dangerous people, Paul warns believers to watch out for dangerous teachings. These teachings may sound good on the surface, but they are rotten at the core and lead us away from Jesus. Children need to be warned not to let anyone move them away from Jesus by unbiblical viewpoints. Children must learn to test everything they hear by comparing it to what the Bible teaches.

Paul warns us not to be convinced by human philosophies that sound good but are false. The word *philosophy* means the search for truth. Paul is concerned in Colossians 2 that human ideas will destroy faith. The rest of Colossians 2 deals with human teachings that lead to ruin (v. 18). Paul does not want unbiblical ideas to deceive us (v. 4), captivate us (v. 8), and disqualify us (v. 18). Notice the progression. It begins with one of the world's lies and ends with abandonment of faith.

Paul mentions three man-made philosophies that had crept into the Colossian church: legalism, mysticism, and asceticism. Ultimately, they are forms of works-righteousness that attack the gospel of Jesus Christ. While the "ism" may change, the outcome will not. If we do not guard our mind, it will capture our heart, and destroy faith in Christ.

Legalism: Paul warned the Colossians to watch out for man-made rules (vv. 16–17). Legalism is the belief that extra rules are needed to please God. In Paul's time, people taught that God wouldn't accept you unless you ate the right food and celebrated the proper religious holidays. They created man-made food regulations and festivals. Legalism is alive and well today in Christian homes and churches. I had a former children's ministry director who would tell students not to drink caffeine, play video games with guns, participate in Halloween, or listen to non-Christian music. This is an example of legalism. She created her own list of rules that do not exist in the Bible and suggested that they made a person holy. The error was subtle because it would only come out in small doses, but the result is that it creates little Pharisees.

Mysticism: Paul told the Colossian church to watch out for "spiritual" experiences (2:18–19). Mysticism is hearing or experiencing the spirit world apart from the Bible and Christ. Paul tells us that a mystical person may pursue a vision or a conversation with angels. Mysticism is popular in yoga, forms of meditation, and the seeking of dreams and visions. I once had a children's staff member at a church who encouraged children to look for crosses and hearts in nature as forms of communication from God. The staff person would invite children to come to the front of the class, tell where they saw the cross or heart, and share what they thought God was trying to communicate to them through this experience. This is a form of unbiblical mysticism that replaces the authority of God's Word with a mystical experience. Paul says mysticism will defraud and disqualify us. It will rob us of the truth by causing us to trust in something that is not true.

Asceticism: Paul warns the Colossian church to watch out for practices of self-denial with the appearance of godliness (2:20–23). There were periods in Christianity when believers thought they were more godly if they slept on hard beds, didn't speak for days, went without sleep or food, or didn't get married (1 Tim. 4:3). The person says to himself, "do not taste, do not touch." This person's life is wrapped up in rules that deny pleasure. Asceticism is a form of works-righteousness that punishes the body by denying forms of pleasure that God has given as good gifts. Asceticism teaches that self-discipline is necessary to please God. Ascetics punish themselves for their sin in hopes that God will not punish them in eternity. While we are to train our body for godliness, we must remember that fleshly discipline adds nothing to our salvation.

The Colossian church fell into the error of believing that Jesus + something = salvation. Many Christians try to combine the world with the Word. Many of us think that Jesus is part of what we need. We believe we need Jesus plus science in order to know truth. We might think we need Jesus plus traditions in order to please God or that we need Jesus plus spiritual experience in order to really know God. The point of the book of Colossians is that Jesus is supreme and sufficient. He is enough.

We need to prepare young people for the counterfeit truth claims they will face. The examples I mentioned came from *within* the church, so we must be vigilant to learn what is being communicated to our children and never assume. We must be diligent to teach God's truth. We should help a child detect false views, debunk claims, and defend against unbiblical ideas. To be forewarned is to be fore-armed. Nancy Pearcey explains why this is important.

"It is not enough to teach young believers how to have a personal quiet time, follow a Scripture memory program, and link up with a Christian campus group. We also need to equip them to respond to the intellectual challenges they will face in the classroom. Before they leave home, they should be well acquainted with all the 'isms' they will encounter, from Marxism to Darwinism to postmodernism. It is best for young believers to hear about these ideas first from trusted parents, pastors, and youth leaders, who can train them in strategies for analyzing competing ideologies."[1]

Young people need to know what the Bible teaches and why it is true. They also must know what the world believes and why it is false. Let us give children reasons to believe Christianity over every other alternative. The best way to drive out a bad worldview is to offer a good one. That is what I will teach you to do in the next section of this book.

PART 3

THE BIBLE'S BIG STORY

How to Teach Biblical Worldview in Four Words

We have covered why worldview is important, what worldview is and how to help a child develop a biblical worldview. In the final section, I provide four outlines you can use to teach a child the big story of the Bible in four words so that a biblical worldview framework is developed.

The Big Story

The Bible is one unified story with Jesus at the center. Jesus Christ is the goal of the Old Testament and provides its true meaning. Any understanding of, and commentary on, the Old Testament that doesn't reveal this fact is at best incomplete and at worst un-Christian. The overwhelming testimony of the New Testament is that Jesus fulfills the Old Testament, which is another way of saying that the Old Testament is about Jesus. The New Testament interpretation of the person and work of Jesus of Nazareth makes no sense if there is no substance to the historical claims of the Old Testament.

Is the Bible a random collection of books or an interconnected book with one main emphasis? Teach the Bible not as if it were sixty-six individual books, but as a single book with a single plot about God's glory displayed through salvation and judgment. If the Bible were a random collection of books with limited connection to one another, there could be no central storyline. The Bible would be reduced to a library of historical documents describing the religious experiences of ancient people while providing moral instruction for future generations.

God uses a tree to capture the big story of the Bible in a single image. A tree reminds us of God's good creation, man's fruit-induced rebellion, Jesus' sacrificial death on the cross for our redemption, and the tree of life in heaven where all things are made new. A tree appears in four important sections of the Bible and is a simple way to teach young people the entire storyline of Scripture centered on Jesus Christ (emphases added):

- *Creation*: "And God said, 'Let the earth sprout vegetation, plants yielding seed, and fruit *trees* bearing fruit' … and God saw that it was good" (Gen. 1:11–12).

- *Rebellion*: "So when the woman said that the *tree* was good for food, and that it was a delight to the eyes, and that the tree was to be desired to make one wise, she took of its fruit and ate, and she also gave some to her husband who was with her, and he ate. Then the eyes of both were opened, and they knew that they were naked. And they sewed fig leaves together and made themselves loin-cloths" (Gen. 3:6–7).
- *Salvation*: "[Jesus] himself bore our sins in his body on the *tree*, that we might die to sin and live to righteousness. By his wounds you have been healed" (1 Peter 2:24).
- *Restoration*: "the *tree of life* with its twelve kinds of fruit, yielding its fruit each month. The leaves of the trees were for the healing of the nations" (Rev. 22:2).

Unfortunately, many homes, churches, and schools only teach a narrow worldview that is limited to rebellion and salvation, but does not concern itself with the broader Christian life and thinking. Discipleship is reduced to conversion while doctrinal truth is downplayed and the application of the Bible for many areas of life is ignored. The big story will help us provide children with the full storyline of the Bible.

I often use my hand to teach these biblical truths to a child. Creation (thumb): God made the world good. Rebellion (index finger): Sin made the world groan. Salvation (middle finger): Jesus paid the penalty for sin. Restoration (ring finger): God will make the world new. Jesus (pinky finger): The Bible is centered on Christ.

Every biblical truth has a counterfeit philosophy that presents a different big story and overarching narrative. Each counterfeit philosophy rejects the biblical truth and presents its own version of the story. If children embrace or absorb a different big story, it will lead them on a trajectory away from Christ. We must have a Colossians 2:6–8 mindset, which teaches the biblical truth so a child becomes established in faith and can dismantle the counterfeit idea in the chart below.

CHRISTIANITY	COUNTERFEIT PHILOSOPHY
Creation	Naturalism
Rebellion	Relativism
Salvation	Atheism/World Religions
Restoration	Materialism/Marxism

How to use the teaching outlines

The four biblical truths in the next few chapters are applicable for a one-on-one Bible study with a child or grandchild, for family worship, to be taught as classroom curriculum in your church or school, or to be used for Vacation Bible School. The first portion of each chapter is commentary so you will understand the topic in greater depth. The bulleted outline is the portion I wrote for use with a young person. We've also created accompanying music, "The Big Story," to teach children biblical worldview so that message, memorization, and music all are integrated; it is available at GospelShapedFamily.com.

I envision parents and grandparents sitting down with a child, reading the Bible, and discussing the truths together. The subject matter is short enough that it could be covered over a weekend away, during a week of family devotions, or spread out over a month. Whatever format you utilize, my hope is that you don't rush through the biblical teachings. Spend time digging deeply into God's Word, discuss the significance of each doctrinal truth, and invite God to work in the heart and mind of your child so there is understanding and transformation.

9

CREATION: WHERE DID THE WORLD COME FROM?

GOD MADE THE WORLD GOOD

A biblical worldview begins with knowledge of God, "The fear of the Lord is the beginning of knowledge" (Prov. 1:7). Nothing can be understood if there is no belief in God, which is why there is a fierce battle around evolution and atheism.

What a child believes about God and his creation are critical elements for a biblical worldview. If the starting point is incorrect, then the foundation is faulty, and all beliefs that follow will be shaped accordingly. The biblical worldview begins with God as he is, not as we want him to be. We can know who God is because he has revealed himself generally in nature and specifically in the Bible.

We can know where the world came from because the Bible provides the true account of history from the beginning of time until eternity.

Belief in the existence of God is critical, but not enough. A child must also understand who God is (Ps. 78:4). All world religions believe in some form of god. What unifies a biblical worldview is the nature and character of God. God, in his redemptive work through Jesus Christ, is the ultimate frame of reference for all other beliefs.

Our view of creation is foundational for a biblical worldview. It is impossible to reject the biblical account of creation and alter the beginning without impacting the rest of the story. If we do not believe what the Bible says about the beginning of history, should we believe what the Bible says about the end of history in Revelation or redemptive history in Christ throughout the entire Bible? The big question for every adult who teaches a child is this: Is Genesis 1–3 fact or fiction? Is it literal or metaphor? These are not inconsequential questions and are monumentally important for the faith of children.

Genesis 1–3 is literal

Train children to believe that Genesis 1–3 is literal and to be understood at face value. Nothing about Genesis 1–3 suggests that it is symbolic, mythical, or written as a spiritual metaphor. If creation in Genesis 1 is not literal, then we cannot believe Adam was a literal person and the biblical explanation of sin entering the world through Adam is also not a literal reality. If we did not fall because of Adam then we have no need to be redeemed by Christ, and the New Testament teaching that Jesus is the second Adam makes no sense, "For as in Adam all die, so also in Christ shall all be made alive" (1 Cor. 15:22).

If we doubt the biblical teaching of six days of creation, where does the skepticism of other biblical teaching end? Let us firmly decide that we will believe the Bible, take God at his word, embrace its literal meaning and teach these wonderful truths to our children so that they can grow up with a firmly established faith that will not be destroyed by the world.

John MacArthur makes the following point, "In an important sense, everything Scripture says about our salvation through Jesus Christ hinges on the literal truth of what Genesis 1–3 teaches about Adam's creation and fall. There is no more pivotal passage of Scripture. What 'old-earth creationists' . . . are doing with Genesis 1–3 is precisely what religious liberals have done with *all* of Scripture—spiritualizing and reinterpreting the text allegorically to make it mean what they want it to mean."[1]

A biblical worldview is shaped by the belief that God created the world in six literal days. Many Christians believe it is inconsequential to believe the world was created in millions of years or in six days. The primary reason why it matters is that it sets a dangerous and destructive precedent for biblical interpretation. When we begin to interpret portions of the Bible as symbolic or metaphorical, it opens the door to interpreting other portions of the Bible in the same way. Were Adam and Eve real people or symbolic? Did the flood of Genesis 6 really happen or was it a literary device? Did the supernatural acts of God in the Bible and the miracles of Jesus actually happen or are they mythical to make a spiritual point? If the straightforward language of Genesis 1 can be explained away as symbolic, why not do the same with other portions of the Bible? Could the resurrection be explained away as metaphorical? Where does symbolism end?

At the heart of the topic of creation are two critical areas regarding the doctrine of the Bible. The first is biblical interpretation and the need to properly understand what the Bible says. Old-earth creationism is poor hermeneutics. It violates basic biblical interpretation rules such as allowing the Bible to interpret itself.

Correct interpretation

A good example of how other portions of the Bible help us to understand Genesis 1–2 is seen in the Ten Commandments. The fourth commandment reinforces that God created all things in six days and makes no sense if the days of creation are not literal. The application of the fourth commandment rests on a literal seven-day week. In the six days of creation, God provided a pattern for humans to follow. Is our need to rest symbolic? Should we spiritualize work? The application of the fourth commandment supports a literal understanding that God created all things in six days.

New Testament treatments of creation speak of the event as a historical, actual event that transpired exactly as Genesis describes it. James 3:9 speaks about Adam being created in the image of God. The apostle Paul believes the account in Genesis 1–3 are literal events. He spoke of Adam being created first, then Eve, as well as the encounter with Satan in the form of a talking serpent (1 Tim. 2:13–14). The Bible speaks about creation as a completed event, not an ongoing evolutionary process that is still occurring (Mark 13:19, John 1:3, Acts 4:24, Heb. 1:2, Rev. 4:11). The Bible is clear that belief in creation is at the very center of the Christian faith, "By faith we understand that the universe was created by the word of God, so that what is seen was not made out of things that are visible" (Heb. 11:3). The correct interpretation of Genesis 1–3 is the one that naturally comes from a simple reading of the text.

Authority of Scripture

The authority of Scripture is the second area of doctrine that guides us in understanding Genesis 1–3. We must ask ourselves, *What authority determines truth? Science or Scripture?* Those who embrace evolution have made science their authority, not the Bible. Evolution is a scientific theory that has no authority, but those who believe in evolution allow it to become the measure by which biblical truth is determined. Should our preconceived beliefs determine how we interpret the Bible or should the clear teaching of the Bible shape our beliefs? Old-earth creationism is not taught in Scripture and is a belief system imported into the Bible. Paul warned the Corinthians not to follow the wisdom of man rather than the wisdom of God's Word and here is a modern-day example that we must guard ourselves against.

The Bible is the perfect account of history and tells us clearly how the world began. Science cannot speak more authoritatively, and we should not allow the wisdom of man to be our guide to understand the Bible. Those who embrace evolution undermine the authority of the Bible at the beginning, thus it is critical to address this with a child because if we begin our journey headed on the wrong path, it will lead us to the wrong destination by undermining the very foundations of faith itself. If you give evolution the throne and make the Bible its servant, you have laid the foundation for spiritual disaster.[2] The Bible is the ultimate test of truth, not science. Children need this essential foundation to build a strong faith in Christ, but sadly, high numbers of churches and homes are not diligently teaching it or robustly defending it.

Naturalism and evolution

Naturalism has replaced Christianity as the main religion in America, and evolution is its central teaching. Naturalism teaches that everything that happens is natural rather than supernatural or spiritual. Naturalism is anti-God and makes no room for the biblical teaching of creation. Therefore, belief in evolution is a matter of faith in which school classrooms and Western culture are pursuing converts from Christian homes with a missionary zeal.

A naturalistic view of life often results in depression, purposelessness, and insignificance. If there is no God and this world is all there is, then there is no purpose to life, no hope for a better future, and no joy other than fleeting pleasures. In addition, there is no standard for truth or morality. Naturalistic societies result in moral disaster because humans have no value and the state has supreme power to do as it wishes.

Evolution is taught as an atheistic alternative to the biblical teaching of creation. Children who embrace evolution have taken the first steps to embracing atheism. Evolution was invented as a way to eliminate God and his commands. Evolution is an attack against God, his nature, and his Word. Those who accept evolution as truth are free to interpret the Bible however they wish and choose whatever version of God they wish. The Bible says that man was created in the image of God. Evolution turns that on its head and creates God in the image of man.

There is a battle for the faith of your child centered around two incompatible views: naturalism taught through evolution and the literal truth of creation in the Bible. Evolution is anti-God, and seeks to usurp the authority of the Bible. Homes and churches that embrace these views are unlikely to remain evangelical. We cannot treat Genesis 1–3 as a myth or metaphor without significant implications for the rest of the Bible and for our faith. As parents and grandparents, we must believe what the Bible teaches. If the biblical account of creation is not literal, then the rest of the Bible is unreliable. Evolution is an ever-changing idea based on mere fancy that has provided no valid reason to distrust the biblical account of creation. The Bible is clear about the creation of the world and all the events in Genesis 1–3; it is trustworthy, and it is applicable to today.

You must teach and defend what the Bible teaches about the nature of God, creation, origins, and humanity. Do not be intimidated or embarrassed to affirm the clear teaching of the Bible. Many Christians have embraced old-earth creationism, trying to harmonize the Bible with evolution, and in doing so are making a grave error that opens the door to doctrinal error in other forms and the abandonment of faith in Christ. Many of these individuals lack the skill to properly interpret the Bible and are simply parroting the teachings of the world and transposing them onto the Bible in a form of historical revisionism. Let us now turn to an outline that you can use to teach children about God and creation.

Teaching children the biblical account of creation

Before anything existed there was God. He is eternal, which means that he has always existed. He is the beginning and the end. We can't understand life or the big story unless we begin with God. God is the creator of the world, the author of the Bible, and the hero on every page. The big story is his story, which is really another way of saying "history." All of history is the unfolding of God's plan for salvation. The four most important historical events to ever occur are creation, the fall, salvation, and restoration.

Genesis 1 begins by telling us that everything exists because God spoke it into existence. The trees, water, animals, planets, light, and humans exist because God created all of them. If you or I were to create something, we would have a reason for creating it, right? God had a reason as well. He created all things for his glory.

The World's Big Lie:
The world came into existence by accident, or evolution.

The Bible's Big Truth:
God created the world and it exists for his glory.

Memory Verse:
"In the beginning God created the heavens and the earth" (Gen. 1:1).

Read Aloud from the Bible:
Gen. 1:1, Col. 1:16, Is. 43:7, and Heb. 11:3

TEACHING POINTS:
Where did the world come from?

God created all things (Gen. 1:1; 31).

- God created the world, and it is very good. God approves all that he made. In the beginning there was no evil.
- The Bible repeatedly declares that God is the "maker of heaven and earth" (Ps. 115:15; 121:2;

124:8; 134:3; 146:6). The world did not begin by evolution.

- God created each of us. We are made in his image and are told to manage creation and multiply on the earth. Every human is valuable and has great worth. The creation mandate gives humans the task of filling, subduing, and ruling over the earth. Man is given delegated authority by God and is responsible to faithfully serve God in the world by stewarding his creation.
- In six days God created the world and everything in it. (Ex. 20:11). Read Genesis 1 together.

Godly people believe God created the world
(Heb. 11:3; 2 Peter 3:5).

- God wants you to believe he created the world, "*By faith* we understand that the universe was *formed at God's command*, so that what is seen was not made out of what was visible" (Heb. 11:3 NIV, emphasis added).
- Peter states that unbelievers "deliberately overlook this fact" (2 Peter 3:5). They do not want to believe in God so they do not believe God created the world.
- The world is a mirror to see God. Creation proclaims the existence of God; therefore, we have no excuse not to believe in God (Rom. 1:20). Psalm 19:1–2 states, "The heavens declare the

glory of God, and the sky above proclaims his handiwork. Day to day pours out speech, and night to night reveals knowledge." Creation is evidence that there is a Creator who is powerful, wise, and beautiful. Creation tells us God exists, but it does not teach us who God is. God gave us the Bible so we can learn who he is and have a relationship with him (Ps. 119:57).

God created everything for his glory (Col. 1:16; Is. 43:7).

- God created everything for a purpose and according to his plan. God created humans to worship him.
- Everything belongs to God and was created for him, "All things were created by him and for him" (Col. 1:16).
- God requires us to live for his glory, which means we are to live in a way that reveals the goodness and greatness of God to others and shows others we love and obey God.

Is there evidence that God created the world?

1. Creation shows evidence that it was designed.

- The heavens declare the glory of God (Ps. 19:1). We see evidence of God's greatness, wisdom, and beauty when we look at his creation.

- Every tree, every bird, every mountain, every baby is evidence that God created the world. Is it possible that a leaf came about without someone to create it? Of course not! Now look around the room. Is it possible that we came into existence without parents? Creation needs a creator. Every leaf and every baby remind us that God is real.
- What we see in God's world agrees with what we read in God's Word. Science and the Bible do not contradict one another. The Bible helps us to correctly interpret what we observe in creation. Any interpretation of the world that conflicts with the Bible is an incorrect interpretation of the world and should be revised to align with the Bible.

2. Creation is complex.

- No one would look at a house or car and conclude that they were the result of an explosion in a metal factory. No one would look at Mount Rushmore and think it was the product of thousands of years of erosion.
- Creation proves there is a Creator. We recognize when something has been created because it shows evidence of being designed.
- To help a child understand the absurdity of evolution, consider doing the following activity.

Write out the alphabet on 3x5 cards with each letter having its own card. Place the cards in a hat or bowl and have children randomly select a letter. Ask the children if, given enough time, it is possible that we could form a series of words that make a sentence and compile enough information for an encyclopedia by randomly drawing letters. Intelligence and order do not come from random nothingness (even the letters that we used to begin this exercise had to come from somewhere).

- What other examples can you find of the complexity of creation? For starters, consider the human eye, the human brain, or the tongue of a woodpecker.

3. Life never comes from nonliving material.

- Living things only come from living things. Babies come from parents, not from nothing. Empty bank accounts do not produce millions of dollars on their own.
- If a tornado travels through a junkyard will it create a fully functioning, perfectly working airplane?
- Evolution is filled with insurmountable problems such as "Where did intelligence come from?" "What holds everything together?" "How could complex, rational life come from nothing?" "Where did energy and matter come from?"

"What is our purpose?" Evolution has no answer for these questions.

4. The universe is finely tuned.

- If there had been slight variations in the universe, then life would have been impossible. Here are two examples:

  - The sun is the perfect distance from Earth. Any closer and Earth gets too hot. Any farther away and Earth is too cold.
  - Ice floats instead of sinks. Ice is less dense than water. It is the only substance to be less dense in its solid form than in its liquid form. If ice were more dense than water, all icebergs would sink to the bottom of the ocean and, because heat rises, the water immediately above the ice would cool and freeze, and, eventually, all of the Earth's oceans would freeze from the bottom upward, killing all sea and lake creatures.
  - What other examples can you find of the finely tuned universe?

5. The Bible does not teach evolution.

- Evolution is contradicted by the Bible. Evolutionary theory claims that through a gradual process and over millions of years one animal turned into another kind of animal. If this were true, we would expect to find this evidence in the fossil record.

- Not one conclusive example has been found. Evolutionists have created the term "missing links" because they lack evidence of animals transitioning to different kinds of animals. They are "missing." Evolutionists point to a few highly debatable examples (i.e., Lucy the monkey), which contain no factual evidence.

- God tells us in the Bible how he created the universe. He spoke it into existence. The differences between creation and evolution are too great to believe in both at the same time.

COMPARE AND CONTRAST	
Key Differences Between Creation and Evolution	
Creation	Evolution
God created the world and everything in it. *(In the beginning God created; Gen. 1:1)*	The world formed from a big bang; chance.
God created in six days. *(On the first day...there was morning and there was evening; Gen. 1:3-31)*	Evolution takes millions of years.

COMPARE AND CONTRAST

Key Differences Between Creation and Evolution

Creation	Evolution
Humans are special, the crown of creation. *(God created man in his own image; Gen. 1:27)*	Humans are not special, just another animal.
Death was the result of Adam's sin. *(The original world was death free—humans and animals were vegetarians; Gen. 1:29-30)*	Death was present before sin.
God created the world good. *(…and it was good; Gen. 1:25)*	There is nothing inherently good about the world.
The world was created in its entirety. *(Universe was created complete; Gen. 1)*	The world became what it is over time.
Your purpose: love, obey, serve God.	Your purpose: love, obey, serve self.

Courageous Conversations:

1. Read Genesis 1 together. What does Genesis 1:1 teach?
2. Does the Bible speak about the days of creation as literal or symbolic? How do we know? How does Exodus 20:11 talk about the days of creation? Why is this important?
3. Read Hebrews 11:3 and 2 Peter 3:5 together. What do these passages teach about creation?
4. Do you believe God created the world? Why or why not?
5. What evidence exists that God created the world?
6. If a person believes evolution is true, what does this mean about right and wrong, the meaning of life, and what happens after a person dies? Why is this significant?
7. What evidence can you come up with that God created the world? (To start, see Psalm 19:1.)

IO

REBELLION:
WHAT IS WRONG
IN THE WORLD?

SIN MADE THE WORLD GROAN

The next important component in the development of a biblical worldview is the state of humanity and an explanation of problems in the world. Evolution offers no explanation for the problems in the world and ends with the denial of the existence of evil.

The existence of evil
A young couple named Jay and Lauren believed that evil was a make-believe concept. They took a year-long bike trip around the world, and while in Morocco Jay Austin wrote on his travel blog,

You watch the news and you read the papers and you're led to believe that the world is a big, scary place. People, the narrative goes, are not to be trusted. People are bad. People are evil. People are axe murderers and monsters and worse. I don't buy it. Evil is a make-believe concept we've invented to deal with the complexities of fellow humans holding values and beliefs and perspectives different than our own—it's easier to dismiss an opinion as abhorrent than strive to understand it. Badness exists, sure, but even that's quite rare. By and large, humans are kind. Self-interested sometimes, myopic sometimes, but kind. Generous and wonderful and kind. No greater revelation has come from our journey than this.[1]

Sadly, Jay and his travel companion Lauren learned that evil does exist and is not a make-believe concept. Because they believed evil was a make-believe concept, they rode their bikes through the terrorist territory of Tajikistan, and five men connected with ISIS stabbed the bicyclists to death.

Humanity is naturally evil because sin entered the world through Adam and Eve and has been transmitted to every person who has ever lived, except Jesus. Good and evil are not make-believe concepts and they are not determined by individual preference but by God himself. If Adam's sin does not apply to all of us, why does the consequence of his sin apply to every human? Death, the penalty for sin, is upon us all. This is evidence of every-one's guilt.

To deny evil is to ignore the evidence that is all around us. All we need to do is turn on the news or surf the web. The doctrine of original sin, the biblical teaching that all humans inherited a sinful state in bondage to evil from Adam, is one of the easiest biblical truths to prove. Any parent with a young child knows the child did not need to be taught to be selfish, to lie, to steal, or to rebel. Children are born as precious bundles of sin.

The fall of man

Our world is full of evil, and Genesis 3 tells us how that happened with clarity. Adam and Eve chose to rebel against God, and their sin impacted the entire created world and plunged all humans into a sinful state. When Adam sinned it resulted in death and judgment for all humans (Rom. 5:12 and 1 Cor. 15:22). The only solution is the redemptive work of Christ (2 Cor. 5:17). Children must be taught the biblical truths of sin, Satan, and God's law.

What is sin?

The Bible teaches that all humans are sinful. Romans 3:23 states, "For all [including children] have sinned. Sin is rebellion (Is. 1:2), disobedience (Rom. 5:19), and wrong-doing (1 John 5:17). We sin when we act as the Lord of our life and live apart from God's rule. All who have sinned are guilty before God, dead in sin, and awaiting God's wrath

(Eph. 2:1–3). The penalty for sin is hell. God is a loving God, but he is also a just God who does not ignore or excuse sin.

The Bible teaches that due to sin, all creation groans and is under the curse of sin. Romans 8:20–22 states, "For the creation was subjected to futility, not willingly, but because of him who subjected it, in hope that the creation itself will be set free from its bondage to corruption and obtain the freedom of the glory of the children of God. For we know that the whole creation has been groaning together in the pains of childbirth until now." All of creation has been impacted by sin. Creation is futile, which means it cannot accomplish the purpose for which it was designed by God.

Creation is spoiled by sin, and humans are in bondage to it. Death, decay, and destruction are the consequences of the sin of Adam's disobedience. Genesis 4–6 describes the moral decline of creation by recording the first murder (Gen. 4:8), polygamy (Gen. 4:19), and culminates with God's declaration in Genesis 6:5, "The Lord saw that the wickedness of man was great in the earth, and that every intention of the thoughts of his heart was only evil continually."

The world rejects the sinful state of man and believes man is inherently good. The world believes that bad actions are a result of bad environment and that the answer is behavior management. Biblically, we need a new heart. The problem is that our heart is a fountain of wickedness. All sin flows from Adam's first sin (Rom. 5:19) and no amount of education, therapy, or government programs provide the solution. The weight of Scripture is that sin is a very serious matter with serious consequences. The penalty for sin is physical and spiritual death. Every person will die physically and under sin is dead spiritually, which is why we need a Savior.

Teach children that the sin of Adam and Eve and the biblical account of the talking serpent is fact, not fiction. The Bible treats this event as literal (Rom. 5:12–19). Jesus spoke of the event as a real, historical occurrence (John 8:44).

Who is Satan?

The Bible tells us that Satan is real, he is God's adversary, our enemy, and the source of evil. God created all things good, including Satan. God did not make Satan evil. The details of Satan's rebellion are provided in Ezekiel 28:11–19. Verse 13 identifies this passage as one that speaks about Satan, "You were in Eden, the garden of God." God created Satan as a perfect guardian angel (v. 12–15). The Bible does not tell us how sin arose in Satan, but it does tell us where sin originated, "unrighteousness was found in you" (v. 15). Sin came from within Satan, which was a choice that he made.

Isaiah 14:12–15 explains the fall of Satan. He sinned when he wanted to exalt himself and "make myself like the Most High" (v. 14). His sin was pride, and God cast him from heaven (Luke 10:18). Satan took a third of the angels with him, who became his servants (Rev. 12:4;

2 Cor. 11:14–15). Satan's rebellion did not surprise God, as he planned for it from the beginning (Rev. 13:8; Eph. 1:4; Titus 1:1–2).

Satan is described in the Bible as a roaring lion who seeks to devour (1 Peter 5:8) and a liar who desires to deceive (John 8:44). He disguises himself as truth (2 Cor. 11:14), yet there is no truth found in him. Satan's tactic is to create doubt and cause confusion. He did this when he asked Eve, "Did God actually say …?" At the heart of temptation is the notion of casting doubt about the Word of God. Satan does this by twisting the Word of God, portraying God as restrictive, with his rules depriving humans of freedom and happiness. Satan attacked God's words and God's character. God is good and wanted good things for Adam and Eve, but Satan twisted those words to cause them to think God was not loving.

Satan lied to Eve by telling her that she would not die and he implied that God was a liar for stating otherwise. Satan lied to Eve by stating that God deceived her, was limiting her pleasure, and taking her freedom. Satan uses the same tactic today. Satan attempts to deceive children with the same lies today by convincing them that happiness is found in self-fulfillment with no consequences. These lies have gone by many different names, but the version that is most common today is called relativism.

Relativism

Relativism is the world's doctrine, which states that right and wrong are determined by community consensus or individual experience. A person with a secular world-view believes that truth is created or constructed, that morality is not based on a determined set of laws independent of the individual, and that the individual is the ultimate determiner of morality. When God's standards of morality are rejected, a new authority must determine what is ethical. Relativism places self on the throne to determine truth. It is another version of Satan's promise to Eve that "you will be like God." This false promise is the seed of all false religion.

The moral code for young people is essentially a morality of self-fulfillment, and that is determined by what makes a young person happy. Self-denial has become the new immorality. Self-fulfillment is the new gospel. Self-discovery is the new method. Exploration and experimentation are encouraged, and any limitation or restriction placed on a child is the equivalent of abuse, as it will not allow the young person to become themselves.

Theology becomes therapy. Sin is a disorder. What a child needs is not discipline, but affirmation and affection. They are not called to repent, but given redirection. The world's answer is soul-care and mental health. The biblical interest in righteousness is replaced by a search for happiness, holiness is replaced by a search for wholeness, and morality by a search for feeling good about self. Christians have unknowingly adopted the same values of culture to the extent that the Christian faith becomes a tool of self-discovery and the gospel becomes the ticket to self-fulfillment.

God's law

Children must be taught that God determines right and wrong and that they are to live under God's authority. G. K. Chesterton once said that God gave us rules so that good things can run wild. God's laws are good. The psalmist says they are delightful, desirable, and sweet as honey (Ps. 119:14; 97; 103). We are to love and cherish God's law.

Moses commands parents and grandparents to teach God's law to the coming generation (Deut. 4:9). In Psalm 78:7, we are commanded to teach the coming generations to obey the law of God so that they will place their hope in God (salvation) and not forget the works of God, but keep his commandments (sanctification). Children of all ages must be taught the Ten Commandments, summarized by Jesus as "love God and love others" (also known as the Great Commandment). God established right and wrong. He is the lawgiver. Children are to be taught to love what is good and hate what is evil (Rom. 12:9).

Satan's tactics have not changed from Genesis 3. Satan still twists God's Word, casts doubt on God's character, and portrays God's commands as restrictive. Contemporary culture has embraced the lie of Satan and believes there are no commands of God to be obeyed. Ultimately, every child must answer the question, *Who determines what is right and wrong?* And, *Is God telling the truth when he says that freedom comes from submission and joy from obedience?* Work diligently to convince your child to believe God's command and obey his authority.

It is important to note that God did not relinquish the world to sin or Satan after the fall of man. The world still belongs to God. Satan does not own the world and has no dominion over creation. He can only steal, kill, and destroy. Psalm 24:1 tells us, "The earth is the Lord's and the fullness thereof, the world and those who dwell therein." God has sovereign control over the world and providentially provided a Savior to restore all things to the pre-fall state. Let us now turn to an outline that you can use to teach children about sin.

Teaching children a biblical account of sin

If God created the world good then why do bad things happen? Why is there pain and evil in the world? Genesis 3 tells us that something went wrong in the world and it is called sin. When sin entered the world it had a devastating effect on everything, including you and me. All creation groans due to sin and awaits being set free. Genesis 3 introduces us to the bad news of sin and the good news found in Jesus.

The biblical story continues with Adam and Eve in a state of perfection in the Garden of Eden where they enjoyed perfect fellowship with God. We are told that they walked with him and talked with him. God gave them one command: They were not to eat of the tree of the knowledge of good and evil or else they would die. Adam and Eve instead listened to the serpent and rebelled against God. As a result, all creation groans under the curse of sin, and every human is born with a sin nature.

The World's Big Lie:
People are naturally good and can go to heaven if they do enough good things.

The Bible's Big Truth:
All people have sinned; this happens when they think, say, and do things that break the law of God.

Memory Verse:
"For all have sinned and fall short of the glory of God" (Rom. 3:23).

Read Aloud from the Bible:
Gen. 3:4–7, Rom. 3:23, 1 John 1:8–9

TEACHING POINTS:

How did sin enter the world? (Gen. 3:4–7)

- God created Adam and Eve good. He gave Adam and Eve free reign in the garden to eat of every tree but one. God told them, "Of the tree of the knowledge of good and evil you shall not eat, for in the day that you eat of it you shall surely die" (Gen. 2:17).
- A creature called "the serpent" entered the garden and convinced Adam and Eve to disobey God. The serpent said to the woman, "You will not surely die … you will

be like God, knowing good and evil"
(Gen. 3:4–5).
- Adam and Eve rebelled against God by
disobeying his command and ate the fruit
(Read Gen. 3:6–7). They sinned against God.

What is sin? (Rom. 3:23)

- Sin is disobeying God's law (Rom. 5:19),
rebellion (Is. 1:2), and wrongdoing (1 John
5:17). God determines what is right and wrong.
- Sin is doing what you want to do instead of
what God tells you to do.
- Sin includes the things we think, say, and do
that are not pleasing to God.
- Romans 3:23 states, "For all [including
children] have sinned."

What happened because of sin? (1 John 1:8–9)

- Sin affects all of us. It separates us from God
(Gen. 3:24) and makes us guilty before him (Is. 59:2).
- The penalty for sin is death and hell (Gen. 2:16–
17). God is a loving God, but he is also a perfect
God who does not ignore or excuse sin. He must
deal with it.
- No one can go to heaven with this sinful condition.
We cannot save ourselves by living a good life or by
doing good deeds (Eph. 2:1–3).

- "If we say we have no sin, we deceive ourselves, and the truth is not in us. If we confess our sins, he is faithful and just to forgive us our sins and to cleanse us from all unrighteousness" (1 John 1:8–9).

Introduction to relativism:

- Relativism believes that right and wrong are determined by community consensus or individual experience.
- Relativism claims that you, not God, get to determine what is true.
- It is another version of Satan's promise to Eve, "You will be like God." God determines what is true and right. He is the lawgiver, and an example is seen in the Ten Commandments.

Courageous Conversations:

1. Read Genesis 2:17 together. What did God command Adam and Eve? What would happen if they rebelled against God?
2. Read Genesis 3:4–7. Explain what happened in your own words.
3. What happened to Adam and Eve when they sinned?
4. Read Romans 5:19, Isaiah 1:2, and 1 John 5:17. According to the Bible, what is sin?

5. Read Genesis 2:17 and 3:24. What does every sin deserve?
6. Read 1 John 1:8–9. What is the only answer for sin?

II

SALVATION: WHAT IS THE ANSWER FOR SIN?

JESUS PAID THE PENALTY FOR SIN

A biblical worldview is based on a life-changing belief in the gospel. The life, death, and resurrection of Jesus is the foundation of a biblical worldview and provides the proper perspective for all of life. The child who does not have a correct understanding of the gospel does not have a Christian worldview.

At the center of a biblical worldview is Jesus, "in whom are hidden all the treasures of wisdom and knowledge" (Col. 2:3). He is of first importance, "I delivered to you as of first importance what I also received: that Christ died for our sins in accordance with the Scriptures, that he was buried, that he was raised on the third day in accordance with the Scriptures" (1 Cor. 15:3–4).

Second Corinthians 5:18–21 explains this aspect as well as any passage in the Bible,

> All this is from God, who through Christ reconciled us to himself and gave us the ministry of reconciliation; that is, in Christ God was reconciling the world to himself, not counting their trespasses against them, and entrusting to us the message of reconciliation. Therefore, we are ambassadors for Christ, God making his appeal through us. We implore you on behalf of Christ, be reconciled to God. For our sake he made him to be sin who knew no sin, so that in him we might become the righteousness of God.

Three points can be made from this passage:

- Jesus came to earth to reconcile sinful humans with God. To be a Christian is to have a right relationship with God in which he exchanges our sin for his righteousness through the death of Christ. Sin must be dealt with. It cannot be ignored or excused.
- Children need to be strongly encouraged to be reconciled to Christ. Paul's specific language is, "We implore you … be reconciled to God." His first concern is the salvation of his hearers.

- God calls all believers to be ambassadors who bring the message of reconciliation to the world. Once children place faith in Jesus, they are to be equipped for the ministry of reconciliation.

Good ambassadors do not make up their own message or alter the message to fit their preferences. Christians are commissioned to proclaim God's message of salvation and to teach God's truth as it was delivered in the Bible. Ambassadors are those who live in a foreign land, serve a different king, and speak a different language. Christians are aliens in this world, serving King Jesus. As God's ambassadors, we are given the authority of the King and we desire to see God's kingdom established. Our mission is to deliver God's message to the world: Repent of sin and be reconciled with God. Our ministry is one of training people to follow Jesus in obedience and grow in Christlike maturity. These tasks are our central duty and should shape our perspective of the world.

Share the gospel

We must share the good news of the gospel with children. The Bible calls children to repent and believe: "Believe in the Lord Jesus, and you will be saved" (Acts 16:31). The Bible teaches that those who reject the gospel are held responsible for their unbelief (John 16:8–9). Salvation is not by works so that no person may boast; it is a gift of God (Eph. 2:8–9). We must encourage our children to believe in the person of Jesus and trust that what the Bible tells us is true. Growing up in a Christian home, going to church regularly, and being exposed to Christianity is not enough. Every child needs to place faith in Jesus.

I want you to read the example of one family so that you avoid their mistake. They raised their child in the instruction of the Lord, but assumed the child's conversion. The brokenhearted mother recalls what went wrong,

> She memorized Scripture verses in AWANA club and learned the books of the Bible, days of creation, and the Ten Commandments by heart. They were beautiful days that passed into gratifying years; and together, we reveled in the joy of learning about our Creator and his creation. …
>
> Fast-forward to my daughter's first year at the university. She came home one day and told me she had watched a film in biology class that showed a whale with legs. I laughed. She didn't. Instead, she said these impossible words, *"Mom, I don't believe the Bible is true anymore. I'm not a Christian."* …
>
> This wasn't a grown child who lacked biblical knowledge or apologetic training. … My daughter had never been reborn. My confidence had been misplaced. … I knew in my head every individual had to repent, believe, and put their trust in Christ personally to be saved. … No amount of Latin lessons, Bible memory songs, or classical literature can do saving work.[1]

"My confidence had been misplaced." That is a powerful statement every parent and grandparent should take to heart. Our hope is not in doing the right things, but in the gospel of Jesus Christ. Let us not downplay the importance of doctrinal instruction, apologetic training, or Christian education. However, they are not substitutes for the work of God to transform the heart.

We must communicate the gospel to our families. Your child needs to hear the gospel proclaimed again and again. We can never overcommunicate the gospel. Let us commit to communicating the gospel and praying that God would open our children's eyes to Christ as the object of faith.

The exclusivity of Christ

Every biblical worldview pillar has a faith-busting alternative offered by the world. The world rejects salvation through faith in Christ because the world does not want to live as God commands. The world knows there is a problem, but does not recognize it as sin. The world presents counterfeit methods of salvation, and we must explain to a child why they are insufficient.

Christianity is different from every religion. Every world religion offers a salvation solution, and each is a works-based replacement for the gospel. Most world religions present God as distant, angry, or uninterested in humanity. The goal of other religions is to appease God through good works or some form of sacrifice. Every religion has a different list of requirements, but for salvation to be achieved, participants must follow certain rules, perform rituals, and/or fulfill requirements that will please their god and earn favor.

Christianity is different because God provided what was needed through Christ to appease his justice. We are not left to do good works to gain his favor. We can never earn our own righteousness. Anyone who tries to achieve salvation through his own efforts will fail and will face an eternity of God's wrath in hell.

The good news of the gospel is that Jesus offers to substitute his righteousness for our sin. The righteousness of God is available to those who believe (Rom. 3:22). Faith in Christ is the key to salvation and involves the affirmation that we are wicked and that there is no hope for salvation apart from repentance and belief in Christ. Some people suggest that Jesus as the only way to salvation is too narrow; they believe that all paths should lead to God. This view is unbiblical. Let us be thankful that God provided *a* way in Jesus Christ. Let us proclaim the good news of the gospel of Jesus Christ to our children and grandchildren.

Teaching children the solution for sin
In Genesis 3 we learned that Adam and Eve rebelled against God by eating of the fruit from the tree of good and evil. Their disobedience shattered their perfect relationship with God, resulting in separation from him and submitting all of creation to the curse of sin. God announced his plan to make things new again by crushing the head of the serpent and sending the Savior through the seed of the woman (Gen. 3:15).

God's plan of redemption unfolds in the Old Testament through Noah, Abraham, Joseph, Moses, and David as they point us to the coming Christ. The flood, Exodus, law, and sacrificial system remind us that the true Savior is still to come. The Gospels open with the proclamation that the Messiah has arrived and that in Jesus all the prophets and the law are fulfilled.

Once again we find ourselves at the base of a tree, but this time it is a cross upon which Jesus willingly suffered and died in our place to pay the price for all sin. On the cross sin and Satan were defeated, and on the third day Jesus rose again, victorious over death. Jesus invites you to submit to him as the King of your heart and the Lord of your life.

The World's Big Lie:
Jesus is a wise teacher, but he is not God.

The Bible's Big Truth:
God sent Jesus to die a substitutionary death on the cross so that whoever believes in him will have eternal life.

Memory Verse:
"For God so loved the world, that he gave his only Son, that whoever believes in him should not perish but have eternal life" (John 3:16).

Read Aloud from the Bible:
John 3:16; 2 Cor. 5:21; 1 Peter 2:24

TEACHING POINTS:

Jesus came to die for sinners (John 3:16; 2 Cor. 5:21).

- God sent his Son so that whoever should believe in him will have eternal life and not perish (John 3:16).
- Jesus suffered and died in our place to pay the price for all our sin (Heb. 9:28).
- "For our sake he made him to be sin who knew no sin, so that in him we might become the righteousness of God" (2 Cor. 5:21).
- Why did Jesus come to Earth?

  - To deliver us from sin (John 1:29).
  - To destroy the power of death (Heb. 2:14).
  - To defeat Satan (1 John 3:8 and 1 John 4:1–3).
  - To fulfill the law (Matt. 5:17–18).
  - To seek and save the lost (Luke 19:10).
  - To serve and to give his life as a ransom for many (Mark 10:45).
  - To reveal God the Father to his people (Matt. 11:27).

Jesus lived a perfect life.

- Jesus was sinless. He was tempted like us, but he never sinned in word, thought, or action.

Jesus was "tempted as we are, yet without sin" (Heb. 4:15).

- He perfectly kept God's whole law. This meant that he perfectly loved God, obeyed his parents, was kind to others, and told the truth.
- Jesus is fully God and fully man. He became a human so that we could be rescued from hell.
- Jesus asked a question you must answer: "Who do you say I am?" (Matt. 16:15–16). Look up the following verses and read each one aloud. Ask a child to summarize whom each person believed Jesus was.

  - Mark 1:1. What does Mark call Jesus?
  - Mark 1:7–8. Who does John the Baptist believe Jesus is?
  - Mark 1:23–24. What did the unclean spirit call Jesus?
  - Mark 8:29. Who did Peter say Jesus was?
  - Mark 15:39. What did the centurion at the cross say about Jesus?

Jesus willingly took our punishment
(1 Peter 2:24).

- "[Jesus] himself bore our sins in his body on the tree, that we might die to sin and live to righteousness. By his wounds you have been healed" (1 Peter 2:24).

- Jesus did this out of love for those who would believe in him. John 3:16 reminds us, "For God so loved the world that he gave his one and only Son."
- God placed the sins of those who would believe on his Son. Jesus suffered, bled, and died in our place.
- Jesus was insulted, ridiculed, beaten, spit upon, whipped, punched, crowned with thorns, and died a painful death on the cross.

Jesus paid for our sin and forgives us.

- Jesus' death completely satisfies God's justice.
- God holds nothing against anyone who believes in Jesus. By trusting in Jesus, our sins are paid for. God took the record of Jesus' perfect life and credited it to us.
- To be saved you must repent of your sins and believe in Jesus Christ for salvation (Mark. 1:15). "If you confess with your mouth that Jesus is Lord and believe in your heart that God raised him from the dead, you will be saved" (Romans 10:9).
- To repent of your sins means that you are truly sorry for your sin. It means you hate sin and want to stop because it is ugly and offensive to God. Instead, you want to live to please God by obeying his commands; this is displayed as we love God and love others.

- Share the gospel message and invite children to respond.

Introduction to world religions

Most people in the world realize there is a problem. However, there are a lot of different views regarding the solution. Essentially, every world religion is a different solution to the problem of sin. Let's review a few of the more popular world religions and the solutions they provide:

- *Islam*: Teaches there is no god but Allah, and Muhammad is his prophet. They believe Jesus is the son of Mary and is a servant of God, but not God himself. They believe the Bible is corrupt and full of errors. Allah prefers judgment over grace. He is far above men and cannot be known. He wants justice more than love. Allah asks his people to make war against infidels. Salvation is obtained by believing in Allah, praying five times a day, giving money to the poor, fasting during Ramadan, and going to Mecca.
- *Hinduism*: Offers many gods under the name Brahman. Hindus believe that people are reincarnated after they die and that what a person comes back as is determined by their actions on Earth; this is called karma. The goal is to achieve enlightenment on Earth so you can go to nirvana when you die. Hindus are tolerant

of other beliefs. What matters is that you are a sincere believer of an authentic religion. They believe all souls will eventually be saved through one of three ways: works (you have followed all the religious rites without messing up); knowledge (you gain knowledge and come to a state of mind in which karma has no effect), or devotion (you become extremely devoted to the gods in private and public life).

- *Humanism*: Looks to people instead of God to solve problems. Man is god. Humanists reject the Bible and worship science instead. God is replaced by man, and evolution is a key belief. Humanism's primary document is called The Humanist Manifesto, which is anti-religion. They use science to answer problems, determine truth, and make the world a better place. Humanists deny God, morality, and salvation in Christ, and they believe in atheism.

- *Marxism/Socialism*: Preaches that life is a struggle between the rich and poor in which the poor are oppressed and have to fight for their rights. Marxists are atheists and believe that God does not exist. Salvation is possible through communism, under which everyone lives in total equality. There is no morality because right and wrong are determined by society. A socialist government takes the place of god.

Our culture teaches that at the core, all religions are pretty much the same. Of course, this is not true. To determine what each religion believes, all a person has to do is ask, *What does this religion teach about Jesus?* This is where every religion differs from Christianity. Christianity believes that Jesus is God. Every other religion believes that Jesus was a wise teacher and a good person who showed us how to live well, but then rejects the biblical teaching that he is God.

You should also ask what each religion suggests as the solution to sin. Every religion except Christianity teaches that you have to do good works to receive God's approval and go to heaven. Each religion suggests there are different good deeds you need to do, but it all boils down to you earning salvation. Christianity is the only religion that teaches it isn't what you have done, but what Jesus did on the cross on your behalf.

All religions other than Christianity are a path to hell. Jesus said that he is "the way, and the truth, and the life. No one comes to the Father except through me" (John 14:6). If anyone ever claims that you can be saved through any means other than Jesus, they are wrong, no matter how sincere they are.

Courageous Conversations:

1. Read John 3:16 and 2 Corinthians 5:21. According to the Bible, why did Jesus come to earth?
2. What did Jesus die on the cross for? Read the following passages:

- John 1:29
- Hebrews 2:14
- 1 John 3:8 and 1 John 4:1–3
- Matthew 5:17–18
- Luke 19:10
- Mark 10:45
- Matthew 11:27

3. Read 1 Peter 2:24. Why is the death of Jesus important? Would it matter if Jesus never died on the cross or rose again?
4. The Bible teaches that Jesus died so that you can have a restored relationship with God and be saved from sin. Do you believe this? Why or why not?
5. Read Romans 10:9. What must a person do to be saved?
6. If you died tonight, how sure are you that you would go to heaven?

12

RESTORATION: WHAT HAPPENS AT THE END OF THE STORY?

GOD WILL MAKE THE WORLD NEW

Hope. It's a word everyone loves because transformation is the deepest desire of the heart. Hope is the great promise of the gospel that Jesus will make all things new. Hope is a future-oriented vision fixed on Christ for the restoration of all things.

Restoration is a theme of Scripture. The word *restoration* summarizes the work of the church and the role of Christians in the world. The Bible tells us that God's plan is for the restoration of the universe to its original good and true state. Consider the following ways the Bible talks about restoration (emphases added):

- *Spiritual restoration.* The Bible presents examples of spiritual restoration occurring when someone sinned against God or others. David seeks restoration due to his sin against God: "*Restore* to me the joy of your salvation and grant me a willing spirit, to sustain me" (Ps. 51:12). Paul encourages mature believers to restore Christians caught in sin. "Brothers, if anyone is caught in any transgression, you who are spiritual should *restore* him in a spirit of gentleness" (Gal. 6:1). Spiritual restoration begins with repentance, which leads to salvation and living in righteousness.
- *Physical restoration.* God cares about us and restores through financial provision and physical healing. "And the Lord *restored* the fortunes of Job, when he had prayed for his friends. And the Lord gave Job twice as much as he had before" (Job. 42:10). God also restores by physically healing our body, "For I will *restore* health to you, and your wounds I will heal, declares the Lord" (Jer. 30:17).
- *Kingdom restoration.* God will make all creation new again, "Repent therefore, and turn back, that your sins may be blotted out, that times of refreshing may come from the presence of the Lord …whom heaven must receive until the time for *restoring all the things* about which God spoke by the mouth of his holy prophets long ago" (Acts 3:19–21).

God is in the restoration business and he has called us to join him. These passages remind us that we are agents of restoration. Paul prays for restoration. He exhorts the church to strive for restoration. He instructs us to restore those caught in sin. Peter states that restoration begins with repentance. He reminds the church that God's promised plan from long ago is the restoration of all things, including a broken world that groans from the curse of sin.

Restoration is a high priority in Scripture, a central aim for the church, and should be important to us. Paul tells the church at Corinth, "Your *restoration* is what we pray for. ... Finally, brothers, rejoice. Aim for *restoration*, comfort one another, agree with one another, live in peace; and the God of love and peace will be with you" (2 Cor. 13:9, 11, emphasis added).

God's plan to restore all things through Jesus

The last element of a biblical worldview that we will explore is the Bible's vision of restoring a fallen world to perfection. What began in Genesis culminates in Revelation. God tells us how the story ends, and it is a message filled with hope. The Bible begins by explaining how all creation existed in perfection and was brought under the curse because of sin. The Bible also tells us that the power of sin was broken, that death was defeated, and that God will make everything new. The gospel of Jesus Christ is the power of God for transformation.

Revelation 21:1–8 provides a hope-filled glimpse of the future Christians can expect. God will restore what went disastrously wrong in the fall. The end of the Bible helps us understand that God's ultimate plan for history is the restoration of men and women from every tribe, as well as all of creation, to the pre-fall state. We are given a glimpse of heaven, the hope of eternity, and the true paradise—and it is exciting! For the Christian, this world is the only hell we will know. For the non-Christian, this world is the only heaven they will know.

A day is coming when God will restore all things to perfect order and eliminate pain and death. Christians live in an already/not-yet tension. God has already claimed victory over sin, Satan, and death, but the consequences of the fall have not yet been reversed. While we wait by faith in God's promised plan for the future, God tells us to be diligent managers who are actively doing his work in the world, knowing that one day he will return and ask for an account of our life. We are to live in light of eternity, recognizing that we are aliens in this world and sojourners who are not to be of the world. Even though this world is not our final home, we are ambassadors of the King who are commissioned to serve him through our work in his world.

God's plan for restoration utilizing Christians

One of the problems in the church today is the failure to grasp the breadth of God's plan for restoration, which includes our personal salvation as well as the restoration of all creation. Biblically speaking, salvation is not the end, it is the beginning. Christians must not stop in the middle of the biblical story. The Bible doesn't end at Calvary. It ends in consummation.

Christ-followers are to live redemptively for the glory of God and the good of the world. How do we do that? Take a moment and consider four questions to determine how God has equipped you to join in his restorative work in the world.[1]

1. What is good in the world that you can promote, protect, and celebrate?

God created the world good, and much of that goodness remains. Christians can promote the sanctity of life, the value of motherhood and fatherhood, a nonprofit cause, or the significant role of grandparents. Christians can celebrate the longevity of a faithful marriage or work to protect freedom of speech, endangered animals, good stewardship of God's creation and so much more.

Christians are often pressured to make their faith private and live it out in the quiet of our own home. As a result, Christianity loses it mission-oriented focus and does not transform culture. Your faith belongs in the public arena of education, politics, social media, and the workplace.

God's expectation is a public faith, lived out in the world for the restoration of all things. Luke instructs us to be salt and light to the world (8:16–18). Paul commands baptism to be public so that Christians can proclaim the gospel and stand for Christ (Rom. 6:3–4). James tells us that faith without works is dead (2:14–26). Matthew encourages us not to be ashamed of God before men (10:32–33).

God sends us as his ambassadors into the world to speak truth, to shape our communities and the culture of our city, to stand for the moral absolutes taught in the Bible, and to engage with the people around us concerning the issues of the day. Christians are to be people who know the truth, speak the truth, and live the truth. Author Philip Yancey notes, "In no other arena is the church at greater risk of losing its calling than in the public square."[2] May we proclaim the gospel and see our work as God's means to restore the world.

2. What is missing in our culture that you can creatively contribute?

God created Christians to be creative. When something is missing, we should find a way to offer it to the world. God is glorified, and the world is helped by properly ordered human creativity. "As each has received a gift, use it to serve one another, as good stewards of God's varied grace: whoever speaks, as one who speaks oracles of God; whoever serves, as one who serves by the strength that God supplies—in order that in everything God may be glorified through Jesus Christ. To him belong glory and dominion forever and ever. Amen" (1 Peter 4:10-11). As good stewards of God's grace, use your gift to serve others. This is one of God's means to restore the world.

Not only did Jesus save us *from* the wrath of God, but he also saved us *for* service to God—to resume the task for which we were originally created. God didn't save us just so we would go to heaven when we die. We need to equip young people to live out God's mission where they live and work. Whatever future vocation a child has must be viewed as a holy calling for the purpose of governing a small portion of God's world and bringing honor to him. Stay-at-home moms, businessmen, teachers, fast-food workers, artists, politicians—every person in every profession needs a vision that they are sent to be a witness to Christ in service to others. Our work isn't something we do for God, but a way to participate in God's work in the world restoring all things.

3. What is evil in our society that you can stop?

God hates evil and so should we. It is a basic requirement of loving our neighbors. Courageous Christians like William Wilberforce, Mother Teresa, and Martin Luther King Jr. have worked to stop evil. Throughout history, Christians have been known for running toward, not away from, the suffering of others, for helping the least, lost, and last as well as standing against injustice in the world. God has called some Christians to be advocates against evil.

When we look at all the problems in the world it is tempting to despair and echo the sentiment of Ecclesiastes 12:8: "Meaningless! Meaningless! … Everything is meaningless!" Rather than despair, however, we can offer the hope of Christ to a hurting world. The gospel transforms individual lives and entire communities. The gospel saves souls, closes abortion clinics, frees women from sex trafficking, increases industry, and eliminates addiction.

The Bible tells us that God will set creation free from its groaning in a radical, one-time event (Rom. 8:19–21). Meanwhile, Christians can bring healing and hope to a hurting world by advocating for good and standing against evil. Christians should strive to bring truth, beauty, and goodness to the world around us. As we do, many will benefit and God will be glorified.

4. What is broken in the world that can be restored? Ultimately, we reflect the gospel most clearly when what has been damaged by sin is restored to God's intended purpose. We live in a broken, messy, sin-stained world, so the list of opportunities is long. Maybe God is calling you to help restore broken homes, broken marriages, broken bones, broken organizations, broken cars, broken hearts, broken dreams, or broken pipes. When God fixes what is broken and we are privileged to be part of it, in a small way we are helping to repair the ruins from the fall and are operating in an important restorative role.

Young people are asking the question, *How do we make the world a better place?* The Bible gives us the answer and the vision. When the gospel shapes why and how we restore what it broken, true culture transformation can occur and result in born-again hearts. The world needs the good news of the gospel and will be blessed by the good works of Christians.

Every Christian is a missionary. Brokenness is the opportunity. Our home and place of work is our mission field. Jesus sends us to our neighbors, our place of work, and our city, where he wants us to make a difference by restoring what is broken and sharing the gospel.

Understanding the creation mandate

The creation mandate is a phrase used to summarize the role God gave us in Genesis 1:28, "And God blessed them. And God said to them, "Be fruitful and multiply and fill the earth and subdue it, and have dominion over the fish of the sea and over the birds of the heavens and over every living thing that moves on the earth." The creation mandate can be summarized with the words *fill* and *form*. God created humans with the specific responsibility to fill the earth by having children and to exercise dominion over the world by bringing order out of disorder. In other words, we are to do what God did when he created the world.

Until Christ returns he has given us joyful kingdom work to do. God created us to be his representatives and to carry on his work on earth. It is critical that children understand their role as God's restorative ambassadors in the world. Ephesians 2:10 provides children with a sense of purpose for life and their future vocation (emphasis added): "We are his workmanship, created in Christ Jesus *for good works*." The apostle Paul tells Timothy that his role as a pastor is to equip Christians "*for every good work*" (2 Tim. 3:17, emphasis added). We have the same role of preparing children for whatever work God has created them for. Selling clothes, driving a truck, installing appliances, teaching children, and managing an organization are not meaningless activities, but services unto the Lord.

Christian Overman helps us understand the application of the creation mandate when he states:

> We were created to govern over the Blue Planet and everything in it. This includes water, air, electricity, sound waves, light, lead, uranium, silver, rubber, maple trees, money, fish, birds, cows, carrots, copper, fingers, thumbs, arms, feet, real estate, sweet potatoes, soybeans and every derivative thereof, including plastic and dyes, as well as digital images, smart phones, e-books, ships, cars, airplanes, glue, paper, antifreeze, pencils, ice cream and cake! Humans were made to rule over whole systems, too, because without systems, governance over things cannot take place: civil systems, legal systems and economic systems are all required. ... This certainly includes bringing the rule of God to bear in our various occupations as we live out the implications of our faith in the context of our daily work, whether it be in the home or the public square.[3]

God created humans to govern all that he created and this has major implications for our purpose in the world. The world belongs to God and he has given us the job of managing it. Our purpose on earth begins with the proclamation of the gospel, but this is not our only responsibility. Overman states,

> When we view the Earth as "God's good creation now broken," and we understand our God-given role and assignment in it, then the Gospel truly is more than the Gospel of our Personal Salvation. It is the Gospel of the Kingdom (the King's domain), which, in fact, is the term used in the Bible to identify the Gospel itself. Yes, it is Good News that my soul is saved from hell. But that's not all there is to the Good News. The Good News of the Kingdom is that Christ restores things as well as souls. What kind of "things?" Earth things!… The scope of Christ's reconciliation extends to the whole of creation, which goes far beyond the human soul. The scope of His redemption extends to all that was affected by the fall, and this is all of creation.[4]

Paul tells us that all things were created by God and for God and that God is in the process of restoring *all things* to their pre-fall state, "For it pleased the Father that in him all the fullness should dwell, and by him to reconcile all things to himself, by him, whether things on Earth or things in heaven, having made peace through the blood of his cross" (Col. 1:19–20). God reconciles us through Christ, but that is not all. God reconciles *all things* that he may have preeminence and he has chosen to use our work as a means toward that end.

Give children this vision. Help them understand that work is a way of fulfilling God's creation mandate; it is a holy calling and a means of loving our neighbor. Martin Luther understood this when he preached, "Christ has served me and made everything to follow him; therefore, I should also serve my neighbor, protect him and everything that belongs to him. That is why God has given me this office, and I have it that I might serve him. That would be a good prince and ruler. When a prince sees his neighbor oppressed, he should think: That concerns me! I must protect and shield my neighbor. ... The same is true for shoemaker, tailor, scribe, or reader. If he is a Christian tailor, he will say: I make these clothes because God has bidden me do so, so that I can earn a living, so that I can help and serve my neighbor."[5]

Running a business, teaching students, managing a home are not secondary activities, but doing God's work in the world. Our vocation is not something we do for God, it is a way to participate in God's work. "There is a common notion among Bible-believing Christians that if a person is really going to serve God, repairing a sewer system can't be compared with the work of a pastor or a missionary. The fact that we can even separate the two in our heads is indicative of the degree of our problem. Yet, as Ray Bakke, in *A Theology as Big as the City*, wrote: "Christians are the only people who can truly discuss the salvation of souls and the rebuilding of city sewer systems in the same sentence."[6] All of our work matters to God and is our contribution to repair the ruins and reverse the effects of the fall. Gospel-shaped work is a powerful restorative force.

Children need a biblical view of how to live in God's world. The creation mandate provides children with a vision for life. It provides meaning and purpose in work and it orients our priorities to be stewards of God's creation. Young people are asking what their purpose in the world is and they want to know if their life has any significance. Children must be given a compelling and biblical vision that work is not a burden, but a blessing and that they are part of God's kingdom mission to restore all things through Christ. Let us now turn to an outline that you can use to teach children about God's plan to restore all things in Christ.

Teaching children about the end of the story

God created the world and called it good. It was not long after this that the problem of sin and the sadness of death cast a shadow over all creation. Under the weight of sin, a good creation turned into a groaning creation. Man's rebellion against God led to wickedness and pain. The result is seen in the pages of history, which are marked with murder, war, greed, selfishness, sickness, corrupt governments, and broken families. These tragic tales are not the end of the story.

The Bible is not primarily a story about the failings of man, but the redemptive plan of God. The Bible is one big story that tells us how God saved undeserving sinners from his wrath through the life, death, and resurrection of Jesus Christ. The Bible's big story is a salvation story based on God's covenant promise. God, in his great mercy, dealt with man's rebellion in Jesus for God's glory and our good. What went horribly wrong in Genesis is reversed at the cross and made new when Jesus returns in Revelation.

The World's Big Lie:
You only live once, so enjoy life while you can.

The Bible's Big Truth:
God gives us hope and promises to makes all things new in Christ.

Memory Verse:
"There will be no more death or mourning or crying or pain for the old order of things has passed away. He who was seated on the throne said, "I am making everything new!" (Rev. 21:4–5)

Read Aloud from the Bible:
Matt. 25:34, 41 and Rev. 21:1–5

TEACHING POINTS:
What happens at the end of the story?

Jesus returns as the reigning King (Rev. 12:17; 20:10).

- After Jesus rose from the dead he ascended to heaven where he is sitting at the right hand of God the Father praying for his people (Mark 16:19).

- A day is coming when Jesus will return to earth a second time to judge all people (2 Tim. 4:1).
- Jesus returns as the warrior King and defeats the dragon just as he promised in Gen. 3:15 (Rev. 20:10). The serpent in Genesis 3 is the dragon of Revelation 12:17. Jesus is the dragon slayer and King of Kings!

All people will spend eternity in heaven or hell
(Matt. 25:34, 41).

- Have you heard the phrase, "You only live once"? It sounds nice, but it's not true. Death is not the end of our story, but the beginning of it.
- God created you to live forever. When your body dies, your soul will continue to live.
- God sends wicked people to hell where they will be tormented forever (Matt. 25:41). God saves those who believe in Jesus to heaven where they will joyfully worship God forever (Matt. 25:34).
- The wise person stores up treasure in heaven, not on Earth, and lives in a way that prioritizes the eternal over worldly things (Matt. 6:19–20).

God will make the world new (Rev. 21:1-5).

- A new heaven and a new Earth will be created. (Rev. 21:1).

- This world is not our final home. We are here on assignment. Our time is short, and life will be over in the blink of an eye (Ps. 103:15).
- God is preparing our eternal home, which is more beautiful and wonderful than we can imagine. Those who believe in Jesus will dwell with God (Rev. 21:2–3). The best is yet to come!
- There will no more pain, death, sadness, or sin (Rev. 21:4). We can be joyful in our trials because we have hope that a better future is coming.

We are part of God's plan to make all things new.

- God didn't just save us from something, he saved us for something—to resume the task for which we were originally created.
- We are to use our gifts, talents, and abilities to repair the ruin caused by sin. Your work is an act of worship to God and a fulfillment of your purpose on Earth, which brings glory to God as you reflect his character in your work.
- Your future vocation is not something you do for God, it is a way to participate in God's work in the world.

Courageous Conversations:

1. Read Genesis 3:15 and Revelation 12:17; 20:10. How is Genesis 3:15 fulfilled in

Revelation? What do the verses teach is the final state of Satan?

2. Read Matthew 25:34 and 41. What is the eternal state for the wicked and the righteous person?

3. Read Revelation 21:1–8. What does this passage teach us about the future?

4. Read Matthew 6:19–20. How should we live in light of eternity? Do your actions and desires reveal that you are living for the things of this world or for eternity?

5. What has caused sadness and pain in your life? How does a relationship with Jesus and an eternal perspective help us through difficult times?

6. Name one thing that excites you about heaven.

7. Do you believe hell is real? Why or why not?

8. Read Genesis 1:28. What gifts and talents do you have that can be used to serve God?

CONCLUSION

Biblical worldview is a set of beliefs about life that determines how we live. A biblical worldview will help children develop a deep and lasting faith in Christ. Every person has a worldview, a way of arranging things in his or her mind. Every child is in the process of organizing his or her views into a pattern that makes sense to the young person. The question isn't *if* a young person will have a worldview, but whether it will be a good or bad one and whether or not the child will learn to bring all of his or her thoughts into obedience to Christ.

There is a battle for the hearts and minds of children, and much is at stake. The world is working diligently to assimilate young people to its way of thinking and living. Alarmingly high numbers of Christian young people are absorbing the views of the world, leaving the church, and walking away from Christ. One of the greatest tragedies of the church throughout its history has been its continual tendency to conform to the culture rather than transform culture through the gospel of Jesus Christ.

We must intentionally nurture, cultivate, and persuade children to embrace the authority of Scripture and the lordship of Christ. The selfish, sinful nature of children means that their natural tendency is to love all the wrongs things. Society is actively trying to persuade children to believe the ideas of today—which places them on a trajectory away from Christ. We must be intentional about shaping what children believe so that they develop a lifelong faith in Christ and serve him.

If you believe these are dangerous times, then you are right. We live in a post-Christian world that is relentlessly working to conform our children to its way of thinking and living. How easy it is to let fear rule our hearts as we face the temptation to shelter ourselves and our kids from evil. How easy it is to condemn ourselves for shortcomings in the discipleship of our children. How easy it is to blame God rather than to trust him as our rock and refuge in time of need. And how easy it is to fix our eyes on chaos rather than Christ. Let us trust in the Lord, for he is the sovereign God who is in control over all.

We must commit to loving God's Word, learning God's Word, and living God's Word. Our children desperately need us to teach them biblical truth, to disciple them to maturity in Christ, to model an imitatable faith, and to train them to recognize and reject the counterfeit ideas of society so they have a firm faith. Will you commit to living in obedience to God's Word by discipling the next generation with a deep, lasting, Bible-shaped faith that will make a real difference for Christ in this world?

Biblical worldview matters. It is worthy of your time and attention. Every child will believe something, based on some authority, that will guide their decisions and direction in life and eternity. Worldview matters because every child is in the process of developing their view of God, creation, sin, hell, salvation, marriage, gender, money, work, abortion, climate change, government, the church, and a long list of other topics. Let us commit to train children to think and live biblically in a secularized world so that we may say, "I have no greater joy than to hear that my children are walking in the truth" (3 John 4).

APPENDIX A:
20 RESOURCES TO DEVELOP
A BIBLICAL WORLDVIEW

Once we understand the urgency of helping young people develop a biblical worldview, the next step is to find the best resources to help with the task. With so many resources available and more written every year, which ones do we utilize? After nearly twenty years of full-time ministry as a pastor, and as a parent of five children of my own, here are twenty of my go-to resources to help young people develop a biblical worldview:

What Does the Bible Say about That?
A Biblical Worldview Curriculum for Children
by Kevin Swanson (grade school)
An introduction to a biblical worldview that will help children make sense of the world around them and show them the big picture of God's truth in the Bible. Presented in a simple, engaging way, this study guide provides a basic introduction to truth, ethics, origins, causality, anthropology, sociology, family, church, civil government, education, economics, defense, crime, and charity. Workbook assignments, games, puzzles, and more are included at the end of each chapter.

Think Biblically! Recovering a Christian Worldview
by John MacArthur

A foundational book every parent, grandparent, pastor, and educator should read. This book will help anyone who is striving to think biblically in today's culture. The book provides models for cultivating a biblical mind-set on worship, psychology, gender, science, education, history, government, economics, and literature as well as confronts the false worldviews that dominate our postmodern world.

My 1st Book of Questions and Answers
by Carine MacKenzie (preschool)

The Gospel for Children
by John Leuzarder (grade school)

Essential Truths of the Christian Faith
by R. C. Sproul (high school)

Every parent and grandparent needs to be teaching children the core doctrines of the Christian faith. There are foundational truths in the Bible every believer, young and old, needs to learn. Each of these books will help you teach the basics of faith in an age-appropriate and easily accessible way. Each book covers key biblical truths that will help young people be grounded in God's Word and guarded from error.

Biblical Worldview Toolkit
by Renewanation (grade school and teen)

A Bible-based and Christ-centered resource to help families, churches, and schools intentionally teach the next generation key truths of Scripture. The toolkit includes approximately ten resources to help you shape the beliefs of a young person so he or she develops a deep, lasting, and culture-transforming faith in Jesus. The toolkit will equip you to integrate biblical truth into your home, church, or school and impress God's Word into young hearts. The toolkit is available at Renewanation.org.

Preparing Children for Marriage: How to Teach God's Good Design for Marriage, Sex, Purity, and Dating

by Josh Mulvihill (grade school and middle school) This book will help you teach preschoolers through high schoolers the truths of Scripture regarding God's definition of marriage, the role of a husband and wife, biblical manhood and womanhood, dating, purity and more. Young people will make few decisions more important than their decision to marry. But they must make other choices before then—decisions about purity, dating, and their roles as men and women. Are they prepared? Our culture is zealous in reaching children with its own views on sex and marriage. Learn how to teach the truth by starting the conversation with children early and returning to it often.

How to Study Your Bible for Kids

by Kay Arthur (grade school)

How to Study the Bible

by John MacArthur (middle school and high school) These resources will help children develop the spiritual habit of reading the Bible, so they can grow as followers of Jesus Christ, and mature in faith. Kay Arthur encourages grade-school children to be detectives and teaches them how to observe, interpret, and apply Scripture based on a study of Titus. John MacArthur provides a concise and readable overview of the doctrine of Scripture followed by suggestions on how to develop a habit of reading the Bible daily.

Keeping Your Kids on God's Side: 40 Conversations to Help Them Build a Lasting Faith
by Natasha Crain

It's no secret that children of all ages are being exposed to negative criticism of Christianity as they spend time at school, with friends, or online. Are you prepared to talk with your kids about how they can effectively answer the tough questions that come their way? This book contains forty of the most common challenges kids face—along with clear, easy-to-understand responses you can discuss together.

The Renewanation Review
by Jeff Keaton and Jen Wooldrige
Kingdom Education: God's Plan for Educating Future Generations
by Glen Schultz

The *Renewanation Review* is a free magazine that promotes, supports, and expands biblical worldview education. It is available at Renewanation.org. *Kingdom Education* will help you capture a biblical vision for the education of children by exploring what the Bible says about the topic. A must read for every parent, pastor and educator.

Roots Kids Worship
by Josh Mulvihill, Dara Mann, and Peter Bourne

Through music, *Roots Kids Worship* teaches children the core truths of the Bible. It is sung by kids for kids with an energy and style that appeals to all ages and is part of an integrated curriculum that combines music, message, and memorization. *Roots Kids Worship* and curriculum is available at Gospel ShapedFamily.com

Answers in Genesis
from Ken Ham

An apologetics ministry dedicated to helping Christians defend their faith and proclaim the gospel of Jesus Christ effectively. Answers in Genesis focuses on providing answers to questions about the Bible, particularly the book of Genesis, regarding key issues such as creation, evolution, science, and the age of the earth. Answers in Genesis has many books and videos as well as two museums worth visiting.

Cold Case Christianity for Kids: Investigate Jesus with a Real Detective
by J. Warner Wallace

Between the ages of eight and twelve, children often start to wonder if Christianity is true. In *Cold-Case Christianity for Kids*, detective J. Warner Wallace draws readers into the thrill of high-stakes investigation by showing them how to think rather than telling them what to think. Detective Wallace gets children excited about testing witnesses, examining the evidence, and investigating the case for Christianity.

Includes author illustrations and links to a website (coldcasechristianityforkids.com) where kids can download activities, fill in case notes, and earn a certificate of merit. Also available is a different version for teens and adults.

Biblical Worldview: Creation, Rebellion, Redemption
by BJU Press

A tool that can be used by schools, churches, and homes to equip high school students with a Christian understanding of all major academic disciplines and cultural arenas. An excellent resource for parents who have a high school student in a public school. Are your students prepared? Are they ready to view the world through biblical lenses? This book will help a young person understand what worldview is and apply worldview to real-life issues as well as to making positive contributions to our world. Apologetics are woven throughout the textbook, equipping students to defend the foundational teachings of the Bible against competing worldviews.

The Christian Worldview Radio Program
by David Wheaton

A radio and online ministry that aims to sharpen the biblical worldview of Christians and share the good news that all people can be reconciled to God through Jesus Christ. The ministry aims at helping believers think and live biblically by focusing on current events, cultural issues, and matters of faith from a biblical perspective.

Evidence That Demands a Verdict
by Josh McDowell and Sean McDowell

An apologetics classic that gives Christian readers the answers they needed to defend their faith against critics and skeptics. The book brings historical documentation and the best modern scholarship to bear on the trustworthiness of the Bible and its teachings. It is a book that invites readers to bring their doubts and doesn't shy away from the tough questions.

Total Truth: Liberating Christianity from Its Cultural Captivity
by Nancy Pearcey

In today's culture, it is not considered proper to mix public and private, or sacred and secular. This division is the single most potent force keeping Christianity contained in the private sphere—stripping it of its power to challenge and redeem the whole of culture. Nancy Pearcey offers a helpful analysis of the public/private split, explaining how it hamstrings our efforts at both personal and cultural renewal. Ultimately, it reflects a division in the concept of truth itself, which functions as a gatekeeper, ruling Christian principles out of bounds in the public arena. Learn how to unify your life, bring all things under the lordship of Christ, and build a robust Christian worldview.

Visionary Parenting
by Rob Rienow

Capture a God-sized vision for parenting that begins by understanding God's purpose for the family and takes an honest look at the current state of the home. The book focuses on understanding and applying God's instructions given to parents in Deuteronomy 6:5–7.

Biblical Grandparenting and Grandparenting
by Josh Mulvihill

What is the role of a grandparent? Learn about culture's misleading messages about grandparenting, get a biblical overview of the role of grandparents, and access groundbreaking research that will give you a vision to impact the next generation for Christ. Includes eight biblical methods to disciple grandchildren. *Biblical Grandparenting* is an academic study for deep readers and leaders while *Grandparenting* is perfect for the casual reader, small group, or class.

Long Story Short and Old Story New
by Marty Machowski

Long Story Short (O.T.) and *Old Story New (N.T.)* are two of the best family devotional books available today. Marty Machowski highlights the gospel in every devotional and helps families read and discuss Scripture in ten minutes a day; the books are suitable for preschool through the tween years.

Jesus Among Other Gods (Youth Edition)
by Ravi Zacharias

In this youth edition of *Jesus Among Other Gods*, Ravi Zacharias gives solid evidence as to why we should choose

Jesus Christ as THE God among all other gods. Zacharias contrasts the truth of Jesus with the founders of Islam, Hinduism, and Buddhism, providing strong descriptions of each faith and solid defenses for the cause of Christ. In addition to the religion comparisons, the book answers questions such as: *What about all the hypocrites at church? How scientific is science? How can you best share what you believe?* and *Does the Bible teach reincarnation?*

The Bible's Big Story
by Jim Hamilton
The Whole Bible in 16 Verses
by Chris Bruno

These books will help you teach a child the big picture of the Bible centered on Jesus Christ. *The Bible's Big Story* is perfect for children while *The Whole Bible in 16 Verses* is excellent for teenagers. Many young people are confused by the Bible and see it as nothing more than a big book of rules or an outdated religious journal of other people's God-experiences. These books will help a young person see the unity of Scripture and follow its main themes from beginning to end.

Also by Josh Mulvihill

Biblical Grandparenting

Equipping Grandparents

Grandparenting

Preparing Children for Marriage

ENDNOTES

Chapter 1

1   The Barna Group, "Changes in Worldview Among Christians Over the Past 13 Years," accessed March 26, 2019, https://www.barna.com/research/barna-survey-examines-changes-in-worldview-among-christians-over-the-past-13-years/.

2   James Montgomery Boice, *Whatever Happened to the Gospel of Grace?: Rediscovering the Doctrines That Shook the World*, (Wheaton, IL: Crossway, 2001), 66.

3   James Montgomery Boice, *Psalms,* An Expositional Commentary, vol. 3 (Grand Rapids, MI: Baker Publishing House, 1998), 977.

4   J.C. Ryle, *Thoughts for Young Men* (Nelson South, New Zealand: Renaissance Classics, 2012), 6.

5   Ryle, *Thoughts for Young Men*, 6–7.

6   National Association of Evangelicals, "When Americans Become Christians," accessed March, 26 2019, https://www.nae.net/when-americans-become-christians/?inf_contact_key=3fe6d503a91e14eb-09034cd02b6b233081cb00e0c63e6f917e88c5746d3481dd.

Chapter 3

1   The Barna Group, "Teen Role Models: Who They Are, Why They Matter," January 31, 2011, accessed December 22, 2018, www.barna.org/barna-update/millennials/467-teen-role-models#.V6tVFjqdLzI.

2   George, Barna, "Parents Accept Responsibility for their Child's Spiritual Development but Struggle with Effectiveness," May 6, 2003, accessed October 11, 2016, https://www.barna.com/research/parents-accept-responsibility-for-their-childs-spiritual-development-but-struggle-with-effectiveness/.

3   Derek Beres, "When and Why Do People Become Atheists. New Study Uncovers Important Predictors," August 31, 2018, accessed October 15, 2018, https://bigthink.com/21st-century-spirituality/study-discovers-how-and-why-and-when-people-become-atheists .

4   Jana Magruder, *Nothing Less: Engaging Kids in a Lifetime of Faith*, (Nashville: LifeWay Christian Resources, 2017), 34.

5   Ibid., 35-36.

6   Josh Mulvihill, *Biblical Grandparenting*: *Exploring God's Design for Disciple-Making and Passing on Faith to Future Generations* (Bloomington, MN: Bethany House Publishers, 2018), 27.

7   Nancy Pearcey, *Total Truth: Liberating Christianity from its Cultural Captivity* (Wheaton: Crossway Books, 2004), 42.

8   John Dunphy, "A Religion for the New Age," *The Humanist* (January/February 1983): 23.

9   Charles F. Potter, *Humanism: A New Religion* (New York: Simon & Schuster, 1930), 128.

10 Gordon H. Clark, "A Christian Philosophy of Education," *Trinity Review,* May 1988.

11 David Wells, *No Place for Truth: Or Whatever Happened to Evangelical Theology?* (Grand Rapids, MI: William Eerdmans, 1993), 248-249.

12 Wells, *No Place for Truth*, 248.

13 Wells, *No Place for Truth*, 11.

14 Larry Fowler, *The Question Nobody Asks about Our Children* (Steamwood, IL: Awana, 2014), 11.

15 Jana Magruder, *Nothing Less: Engaging Kids in a Lifetime of Faith* (Nashville: LifeWay Christian Resources, 2017), 104-105.

16 Magruder, *Nothing Less*, 104-105.

17 Christian Smith, *Lost in Translation: The Dark Side of Emerging Adulthood* (New York: Oxford University Press, 2011), 11.

Chapter 4

1   J.C. Ryle, *Old Paths: Being Plain Statements on Some of the Weightier Matters of Christianity* (Public Domain, 2013), 12-13.

2   Ryle, *Old Paths*, 14.

Chapter 5

1   Robert B. Brandom, *Rorty and His Critics* (New Jersey: Wiley-Blackwell, 2000), 22.

2   Josh McDowell, *The New Evidence That Demands a Verdict* (Nashville: Thomas Nelson Publishers, 1999), 4–7.

3   Nelson Glueck, *Rivers in the Desert: A History of the Negev* (New York: Farrar, Strauss, and Cudahy, 1959), 31.

4   William F. Albright, *Archaeology and the Religion of Israel* (Baltimore: John Hopkins, 1953), 176.

5   John Warwick Montgomery, *History and Christianity* (Downers Grove: Intervarsity Press, 1971), 29.

6   Bernard Ramm, *Protestant Christian Evidences* (Chicago: Moody Press, 1953), 230-231.

7   McDowell, *The New Evidence*," 34-38.

8   Roland H. Bainton, *Here I Stand: A Life of Martin Luther* (New York: Mentor, 1955), 144.

Chapter 6

1   The Barna Group, "A Biblical Worldview Has a Radical Effect on a Person's Life," accessed March 26, 2019, https://www.barna.com/research/a-biblical-worldview-has-a-radical-effect-on-a-persons-life/.

2   James Montgomery Boice, "The Suffiency of the Word of God," Sermon, May 23, 1993, Tenth Presbyterian Church, https://www.tenth.org/resource-library/articles/the-sufficiency-of-the-word-of-god.

Endnotes

3 John MacArthur, *Think Biblically! Recovering a Christian Worldview* (Wheaton: Crossway, 2003), 22.

4 Jana Magruder, *Nothing Less: Engaging Kids in a Lifetime of Faith*, (Nashville: LifeWay Christian Resources, 2017), 22-24.

5 MacArthur, *Think Biblically!*, 22.

6 Harry Ironside, *Studies on Book One of the Psalms* (Neptune, N.J.: Loizeaux, 1952), 112.

7 Charles Spurgeon, *The Treasury of David*, Psalms 1–26, vol. 1a (Grand Rapids: Zondervan, 1968), 269.

Chapter 7

1 Jana Magruder, *Nothing Less: Engaging Kids in a Lifetime of Faith*, (Nashville: LifeWay Christian Resources, 2017), 49–51.

2 Magruder, *Nothing Less,* 74.

3 Relevant Magazine, "Research: Only 17% of Christians Actually Have a Biblical Worldview," May 11, 2017, accessed January 25, 2019, https://relevantmagazine.com/slice/research-only-17-of-christians-actually-have-a-biblical-worldview/.

4 Woodrow Kroll, "The New America and the New Bible Illiteracy," June, 27, 2007, accessed September 27, 2018, http://freerepublic.com/focus/f-religion/1857058/posts

5 Kroll, "The New America."

6 Kroll, "The New America."

7 Alex McFarland and Jason Jimenez, *Abandoned Faith: Why Millennials are Walking Away and How You Can Lead Them Home* (Illinois: Tyndale House, 2017), 29.

Chapter 8

1 Nancy Pearcey, *Total Truth: Liberating Christianity from Its Cultural Captivity* (Wheaton: Crossway Books, 2004), 126.

Chapter 9

1 John MacArthur, *Think Biblically! Recovering a Christian Worldview* (Wheaton: Crossway, 2003), 62.

2 John MacArthur, *Think Biblically!*, 68.

Chapter 10

1 Hank Berrien, "American Couple Believing Evil is a Make-Believe Concept Bike Through Territory Near Afghan Border. ISIS Stabs Them to Death," accessed August 16, 2018, https://www.dailywire.com/news/34581/american-couple-believing-evil-make-believe-hank-berrien.

Chapter 11

1 Scarlett Clay, "Homeschool Will Not Save Them," Desiring God, March 7, 2018, https://www.desiringgod.org/articles/homeschool-will-not-save-them.

Chapter 12

1 John Stonestreet and Warren Cole Smith, *Restoring All Things: God's Audacious Plan to Change the World through Everyday People* (Grand Rapids: Baker Books, 2015), 25–26.

2 Philip Yancey, *Christians and Politics: Uneasy Partners* (Nashville: Creative Trust Digital, 2012).

3 Christian Overman, "The Lost Purpose of Learning," August 21, 2016, issuu.com, accessed November 3, 2018, https://issuu.com/christianoverman/docs/the_lost_purpose_for_learning.docx.

4 Overman, "The Lost Purpose of Learning."

5 Martin Luther, "Sermon in the Castle Church at Weimar," in *D. Martin Luthers Werke: Kritische Gesamtausgabe*, vols. 60 (Weimar: Herman Böhlaus Nachfolger, 1883–1980), 382.

6 Overman, "The Lost Purpose of Learning."